WAGING PEACE
The Story of Jane Addams

WAGING PEACE
The Story of Jane Addams

Peggy Caravantes

620 South Elm Street, Suite 223
Greensboro, North Carolina 27406
http://www.morganreynolds.com

WAGING PEACE: THE STORY OF JANE ADDAMS

Copyright © 2004 by Peggy Caravantes

All rights reserved.

Library of Congress Cataloging-in-Publication Data

Caravantes, Peggy, 1935-
   Waging peace : the story of Jane Addams / Peggy Caravantes.
      p. cm.
   Includes bibliographical references and index.
   ISBN 1-931798-40-0 (library binding)
   1. Addams, Jane, 1860-1935—Juvenile literature. 2. Women social reformers—United States—Biography—Juvenile literature. I. Title.
   HV28.A35C37 2004
   361.92—dc22

                          2004008357

Printed in the United States of America
First Edition

World Writers

To my sisters-in-law Gloria, Marcia, and Patty—
for letting me have your brother

Contents

Jane Addams (1860-1935)
(Courtesy of the Library of Congress.)

Chapter One

Young Jane

Jane Addams was born at a time of great flux, seven months before the beginning of the American Civil War. After four years of violent battles and devastation, the country would reunite, slavery would be done away with, and the United States would enter into a period of rapid industrial development.

The following decades would see thousands of Americans fleeing their farms and small towns to crowd into cities such as Chicago and New York, where they would be joined by millions of immigrants from Europe and Asia. The burgeoning cities were not equipped to handle such an influx though, and federal, state, and local governments were slow to enact programs to help the urban poor avoid lives of misery and deprivation.

Jane Addams dedicated her life to solving the social problems created by the rapid industrialization and surge in immigration. Later in life, she would turn her attention to international affairs and strive to end the wars that consumed much of the world during the first half of the twentieth century. In the process, she would become a world-famous and highly controversial figure.

Jane Addams was born on September 6, 1860 to John and Sarah Addams of Cedarville, Illinois. She was a frail child who suffered from a form of tuberculosis called Pott's disease that settled in her spine and caused it to curve. This resulted in her having to hold her head to one side and to walk pigeon-toed. Her pale face, deep-set gray eyes, and thin body added to her sickly appearance. The family pampered Jane, reacting to the least sign of illness with immediate attention.

When Jane was only seven months old, the South seceded from the Union. Jane's father, John Addams, had served in the Illinois State Legislature for years. While in the state capital in Springfield, he had befriended a lawyer and politician named Abraham Lincoln. Before Lincoln was elected president, the two men corresponded frequently. Lincoln always addressed his letters to "My dear Mr. Double-D-ed Addams." Jane's father held Lincoln in the deepest respect and when the Civil War began he raised enough money to outfit an Illinois regiment called the Addams Guards.

Jane's mother, Sarah Addams, was a strong woman who was talented at music and drawing. The daughter of a wealthy Pennsylvania family, she moved with her new husband to the undeveloped prairie state of Illinois in 1844. They eventually settled on Cedar Creek, north of Chicago. John bought a six-year-old flourmill and a sawmill with eighty adjoining acres. The couple moved

The Addams family home. *(Courtesy of University of Illinois at Chicago, University Library, Jane Addams Memorial Collection.)*

into a two-room house on the property. On a hillside John planted a bit of their home state of Pennsylvania—Norway pine tree seeds that he had brought with him. Those trees took root in the rich soil and soon grew strong and tall. They were planted to serve a practical purpose as a windbreak, but they also had symbolic value. Their thick limbs and rustling needles reminded the Addams family that, with the nourishment of the earth and plenty of water and sunlight, even the tiniest seed could grow. And, like the Norway pines, the Addams family thrived in this new land.

Ten years after arriving in Illinois, John built a two-story gray brick house across the street from his busy mills. The town of Cedarville developed around the mills. He helped establish the first school, the first church,

and the first library in town—the library initially operated out of his home. He took the lead in bringing the
railroad to northern Illinois. John Addams was elected to
the Illinois State Senate as a member of the Whig Party
the same year he built his new home. The following year
he helped to establish the Republican Party and was re-
elected to the State Senate seven times as a Republican.

Sarah managed the large household and at times ran
the family business when her husband was in Springfield. She churned butter, baked bread, made soap, molded
candles, sewed the family's clothes, and stitched quilts.
She cooked three meals a day for the family and for
twenty workers at the mills. Her only assistance came
from the family servant Polly and a couple of hired girls.
Sarah worked up until the last days of all nine of her
pregnancies. The first eight were relatively easy births,
but the ninth proved to be more troublesome.

Sarah Addams always helped a neighbor in need.
Even though she was seven months pregnant with her
ninth child, and forty-six years old, she went to help a
wagon maker's wife who had gone into labor. The only
doctor in the village was away and Sarah stayed to help
with the delivery. Afterward, Sarah collapsed, went into
convulsions, and had to be carried home. Her baby, born
prematurely, died soon after birth. A week later, on
January 14, 1863, Sarah looked at her husband, repeated
the Lord's Prayer, and died. The family buried Sarah and
the baby next to the graves of three of her other children—Georgiana, Horace, and George.

After Sarah's death, Jane's oldest sister, seventeen-year-old Mary, assumed her mother's role. She managed the household and supervised the younger children—Jane, age two; Alice, nine; Weber, ten; and Martha, eleven.

When Jane was almost five years old, she walked into her father's study one day and found him crying. She did not expect to see tears in her strong father's eyes. In his

Jane's beloved father, John Addams. *(Courtesy of University of Illinois at Chicago, University Library, Jane Addams Memorial Collection.)*

hands he held a thin, treasured packet of letters that had been written by his good friend Abraham Lincoln, whose portrait hung on the wall. Now Lincoln was dead—assassinated by John Wilkes Booth on April 14, 1865, at Ford's Theater in Washington, D.C.

In 1867, when Jane was seven years old, John Addams married a widow, Anna Haldeman. Anna had two sons, eighteen-year-old Harry, who was studying medicine, and George, six months younger than Jane. Because her two sisters and brother were so much older, George became Jane's playmate. They played chess, climbed hills, searched caves, and collected flowers, leaves, and walnuts. When they tired of building hills of wet bran and watching the waterwheel turn at the Addams flourmill, they would sneak rides on the huge logs that drifted down Cedar Creek to the sawmill. On rainy days, they went to an abandoned limekiln and performed plays they had made up together. With a green feather in his hat and a green wooden sword, George loved to play the part of "The Knight of the Green Plume." Jane performed all the other roles. One day George used his painted sword to challenge a muskrat swimming in the creek. The muskrat fastened its teeth onto his hand, refusing to let go, until Jane and another friend cut off its head and pried open its jaw to free George.

Most of their days were happy and carefree. As an adult, Jane believed that all children should have such untroubled childhoods. In later years it saddened her to see the children in Chicago's slums playing in the busy streets. As they dodged pedestrians and traffic, she wished they could experience wide-open land, sunshine, fresh air, flowers, and trees.

Jane and George attended the one-room village school. Although Jane, an excellent student, liked English and Latin best, she wanted to pursue what George was interested in as well. He liked nature, biology, and scientific experiments. When George stated his intention to become a doctor, Jane decided she would also have a medical career.

Jane loved her stepbrother, but adjusting to her new stepmother was not so easy. Anna Haldeman Addams was most interested in society, proper dress, good man-

Jane, Anna Addams, and George Haldeman. *(Courtesy of University of Illinois at Chicago, University Library, Jane Addams Memorial Collection.)*

ners, and literature. She enjoyed attending parties and entertaining friends, but also made a point of sharing her love of reading with the younger children. After dinner each evening, she read them Shakespeare's plays, taking all of the parts herself.

Anna Addams, who lived to be ninety-three, had a quick temper. She ran a strict household and expected the children to conform to her rules. She was also an accomplished musician who played the guitar and often sang to entertain family and friends. Even though Jane's stepmother did not spoil Jane, as her father and older siblings tended to do, Jane eventually grew fond of the new Mrs. Addams and even called her "Ma."

Mrs. Addams did not approve of Jane's pursuing a medical career, but she did encourage Jane to think for herself. Mrs. Addams also balanced Jane's reading list by encouraging her to read more fiction, such as Louisa May Alcott's *Little Women,* along with the heavy volumes of history and biography that were recommended by her father.

Jane loved spending time with her father. She wanted to be just like him. She even rubbed her index finger against her thumb over and over in an attempt to develop the flattened 'miller's thumb,' which came from her father's constant rubbing to determine the flour's quality. Jane copied his practice of writing in a diary each day and of reading widely. She read classic literature, biographies, and *A History of the World.* Her father encouraged her reading by paying her small sums of money for completing certain works.

Everyone who dealt with John Addams recognized his integrity. After his death years later, the *Chicago Times* stated that although many state legislators had likely refused bribes, John Addams was the only one to whom a bribe was never even offered. Jane wanted to incorporate this same honesty in her life. If she ever told a lie, she would toss and turn all night, unable to sleep because of it.

One night she lay awake, worrying about a lie she had told that day. Her imagination held her "in the grip of a

Young Jane Addams. *(Courtesy of The Jane Addams Collection, Swarthmore College Peace Collection.)*

miserable dread of death, a double fear, first, that I myself should die in my sins and go straight to that fiery Hell which was never mentioned at home, but which I had heard all about from other children, and second that my father—representing the entire adult world which I had . . . deceived—should himself die before I had time to tell him."

Finally, Jane could bear her deceit no longer. She decided to go downstairs and confess to her father. At the bottom of the staircase, she hesitated—she was afraid to walk by the unlocked front door and cross the dark living room. Her need to confess outweighed her fear, however, and she arrived breathless at her father's bedside. After hearing her confession, he assured her that if he "had a little girl who told lies," he was glad that she "felt too bad to go to sleep afterward."

Her father's religious beliefs also influenced Jane. John Addams did not align himself with a particular religious denomination, preferring instead to attend several different churches and to offer financial support to all of them. When pressed, Addams would describe himself as a Hicksite Quaker, meaning a Quaker who followed the teachings of Elias Hicks. Hicks believed in the authority of what Quakers call the "inner light," which means, among other things, a commitment to personal integrity, charity, religious tolerance, and democracy in church and state. Some Hicksite Quakers were accused of denying the authority of the Bible because they placed emphasis on the individual's inner light as well as the written text, but John Addams taught a large Bible study class for young people. Jane regularly attended Sunday school to learn about leading a Christian life, but she was not baptized until adulthood.

Jane's high school graduation photo. *(Courtesy of University of Illinois at Chicago, University Library, Jane Addams Memorial Collection.)*

When John Addams remarried, his oldest daughter Mary, who had taken care of the younger children since their mother's death, left home to study music and china painting at Rockford Female Seminary. Rockford was designed to prepare its students for fields of usefulness—generally, this was interpreted to mean missionary work. The school was given permission to grant bachelor's degrees in 1847, but its leaders preferred to remain a seminary and the first degrees were not awarded until 1882. It was unusual for women to attend institutes of higher education during this time—John Addams was unique in having the money and the willingness to send all four of his daughters to college.

The first Addams sister to attend Rockford had been Jane's older sister Martha. Soon after she arrived at the seminary, Martha drank water from a contaminated well, contracted typhoid, and died. The suddenness of her death scared Jane—coupled with her mother's death, Martha's demise left Jane even more insecure and alone. When Mary followed Martha to Rockford, Jane became terrified that the sister who had raised her would also die.

But Mary did not die. She survived Rockford Seminary and fell in love with a Presbyterian minister, John M. Linn. Eight years after John Addams married Anna, Mary and John Linn were wed. The family was delighted. A few years after that, Jane's sister Alice and their stepbrother Harry Haldeman announced their engagement—news that was met with objections from both sides of the family. Alice and Harry were not related by blood so there were no legal obstacles to their union, but some members of the Addams family thought it was inappropriate for two people who had been raised together to be married. The lovers were determined, however, and proceeded with their plans. John Addams initially said he would not attend the wedding, but relented at the last minute and gave the newlyweds his blessing.

Jane's family had its share of sorrows, but on the whole her life was a privileged one. Her first encounter with real poverty came on a trip to Freeport, a town near the flourmill, when her father conducted some business in one of the shabbier areas, called Kilgrubbin. There, poor Irish immigrants—many of them refugees from the devastating potato famine of the 1840s—lived in tumbledown shacks resting on logs that were stacked to protect them from floods.

Jane, who had never seen poverty up close before, asked her father "why [do] people [live] in such horrid little houses so close together?" When he explained that not all people enjoyed the privileges their family had, Jane declared that when she grew up, she would have a very large house. Rather than building next to other big houses in a wealthy part of town, Jane said she would build her house in a neighborhood like Kilgrubbin, so that she could share it with the poor people.

One Sunday, Jane proudly modeled a new coat for her father's approval before they left for church. Her father gently suggested that Jane might want to wear her old coat to church since it would keep her just as warm and would not shame the children who could not afford such a pretty coat. From a young age, Jane was taught about the differences between the rich and the poor. She also learned the value of hard work. These were two traits she would carry into adulthood.

Chapter Two

Hearing Her Call

In 1877, when she was seventeen, Jane followed in her sisters' footsteps by enrolling at Rockford Seminary. She had wanted to attend Smith College, where she could obtain a bachelor of arts degree. She passed Smith's difficult entrance exams, but John Addams was a trustee for Rockford and wanted her to go to the same school her sisters had attended. He believed that completion of the course at Rockford followed by a couple of years touring Europe was the appropriate education for a young woman.

Life at Rockford followed a strict pattern. The day started when a bell rang at 6:30 A.M. Breakfast followed at seven. The girls were required to spend an hour a day doing household chores. After the morning meal, the students cleaned their own rooms, including taking care of the linens and dishes they brought from home. Each girl also cleaned the stove used to heat her room after it cooled from the fire she had built the night before. Everyone attended weekly prayer meetings, church, Sunday school, and daily chapel.

Despite the regimentation, Jane enjoyed her years at Rockford. She was popular with the other girls and was elected class president. She developed many close friendships and became particularly close to Ellen Gates Starr, a farmer's daughter. But after only one year at Rockford, Ellen had to drop out because her family could no longer afford the cost. She became a teacher at the Kirkland School for Girls in Chicago. Even though they were no longer in school together, Jane and Ellen remained close and corresponded frequently.

Rockford's stated purpose was to send women into fields of usefulness. Principal Anna P. Sill interpreted this to mean preparing them to be missionaries or to be the wives of missionaries. Almost from the first, Jane and Miss Sill clashed. Jane knew that Rockford's original charter gave the school the authority to award bachelor's degrees. In her thirty-year tenure at Rockford, Anna Sill had chosen not to offer degrees to her students. She thought of Rockford as a religious training school. Jane hoped to change that notion.

In preparation for the possibility of receiving a degree, Jane took higher math and science courses as well as Latin and Greek. Despite the time and effort required by the more challenging course of study, she remained at the top of her class. Her religious training proved to be more difficult. Anna Sill knew that Jane had not been baptized and was determined to convert her. Every day in chapel she led the entire student body in prayer for those who had not yet come into the fold. Although she did not say Jane's name out loud, everyone knew to whom she referred. But Jane did not want to lead the rough, rugged life of a foreign missionary. She worried her fragile health would not be up to such hardships. She resisted her principal's conviction that her future had to be decided right away. Jane was not yet sure what she wanted to do.

Jane wrote for the *Rockford Seminary Magazine.* In her senior year, she was selected as editor. When Rockford became the first women's school accepted into the Interstate Oratorical Contest (a debate competition) in Jacksonville, Illinois, Jane's classmates chose her to represent them. One of the other entrants was William Jennings Bryan from Illinois College. At the turn of the century, he would become a three-time presidential candidate who was renowned for his dramatic and compelling speeches. But in this contest, neither he nor Jane won. Bryan placed second; Jane was fifth.

As graduation neared, Jane began to worry. All the other girls seemed to have definite plans. Most of them would marry or become missionaries. Jane knew that she wanted to help those less fortunate but she did not know how. She finally decided that, because doctors take care of people, she would apply to Woman's Medical College of Pennsylvania, in Philadelphia. She had a vague notion that such a career path might fulfill her need to help others. Jane and her father clashed about her attending medical school. When Jane delivered the valedictory address at Rockford's graduation ceremonies, she aimed her remarks at her father as she talked to the audience of the importance of encouraging a woman's potential.

Jane, with parasol, at Rockford. *(Courtesy of University of Illinois at Chicago, University Library, Jane Addams Memorial Collection.)*

Jane received a certificate of completion at graduation—not a degree—and returned to Cedarville for the summer. She was twenty-one years old but still not sure about her future. This indecisiveness would last for another eight years.

Though Jane had planned to attend medical school in the fall, by July she had changed her mind. Her best friend in Cedarville, Flora Guiteau, needed her more.

Flora had a half-brother, Charles Julius Guiteau, who

suffered from mental illness. That summer, he became very upset over his inability to get elected to a public office. On July 2, 1881, he shot President James A. Garfield at a railroad station in Washington, D.C. Mortally wounded, the president lingered for weeks before he died on September 19.

The people of the United States were outraged. Flora and her family were humiliated and ostracized. Despite the outpouring of anger towards the Guiteaus, Jane stood by Flora. She stayed with her and even read aloud to her on the day her brother was hanged. The tragedy affected the entire Addams family: Flora had been a frequent guest in their home and her father worked for Mr. Addams.

To distract his family, John Addams decided to combine business and pleasure by taking them on a vacation trip to northern Michigan. He planned to inspect some copper mining properties for possible purchase. On the trip, Mr. Addams became ill and doubled over with pain. The family rushed him to a hospital in Green Bay, Wisconsin, where doctors diagnosed acute appendicitis. Within thirty-six hours, at the age of fifty-nine, he was dead of a ruptured appendix. The stunned family returned to Cedarville and buried John Addams next to Jane's mother, Sarah, under the Norway pines he had planted when he first came to Illinois.

Jane had always depended on her father's guidance and now she wrote to her friend Ellen Starr: "The greatest sorrow that can ever come to me has passed, and I hope it is only a question of time until I get my moral purposes straight." She had lost her mother, a sister, and now her beloved father. She felt rootless and alone.

Though her family still opposed her decision to attend medical school, Jane felt more strongly than ever that she needed to continue on that course. Her father's death made her conscious of her own mortality. It also made her want to be a person he would be proud of. Her stepbrother, George, had already gone east to study medicine at Johns Hopkins University. Anna Addams decided to close the house in Cedarville and go with Jane to Philadelphia.

In October 1881, Jane started medical school. She attended for seven months. She passed all of her courses, but did not like the school or the curriculum. Her unhappiness was compounded by the demands that Anna Addams placed on her to participate in society. Jane's health suffered under the strain of attending medical school while trying to satisfy her stepmother's demands that she behave like other young women of her social class. Though John Addams had died without a will, by law one-sixth of his estate went to each of his four surviving children. The money made Jane independently wealthy, but she could not imagine using it to strike out on her own—young ladies simply did not do such things.

The stress affected Jane's health. She even spent time in a Philadelphia hospital with severe back pain. Eventually, she and Anna Addams returned to Cedarville. Despite her health problems, Jane forced herself to go back for that year's graduation ceremonies at the renamed Rockford College for Women. Rockford had finally decided to give academic degrees to those who qualified.

Because Jane had taken extra coursework while attending Rockford, she met the requirements. She received her long-awaited bachelor of arts degree at the 1882 ceremony. Her 1881 certificate had been awarded to Laura Jane Addams, her 1882 degree to Jane Addams—the name she used for the rest of her life.

Although she would receive fourteen honorary degrees in her lifetime, none held as much meaning for her as this first degree from Rockford. In honor of her studies, Jane donated $1,000 of her own money for the purchase of science books for the school.

At the age of twenty-two, Jane received her first marriage proposal. It came from her stepbrother, George. Because they had been very close as children, Jane thought of George as a brother, not a potential husband. Still, she felt pressured to accept his proposal. Jane's life had been unusual enough already—she had gone to college and even had a year of medical school. Perhaps it was time for her to settle down.

Though she could not say exactly why, Jane resisted marriage. She wanted to do something important with her life but was frustrated at her lack of direction. The pressure made her sick. By winter she was almost an invalid and spent several months in bed. Family and friends convinced her it was time to seek help.

Jane decided to go to Mitchellville, Iowa, to see her sister Alice and her stepbrother/brother-in-law Harry Haldeman, who was now a doctor. Haldeman performed successful, but difficult, surgery on Jane's spine. For six months she had to lie flat on a board while scar tissue

Jane soon after spine-straightening surgery. *(Courtesy of University of Illinois at Chicago, University Library, Jane Addams Memorial Collection.)*

grew and pulled her spine straight. Then Haldeman fashioned a heavy brace, styled like a straitjacket, out of steel and whalebone. It fit down to Jane's hips and acted as a crutch under her arms to remove pressure from her spine. It came so high in front that it pressed on her lungs. Jane had to wear this uncomfortable apparatus for more than a year. The surgery also left her unable to bear children.

When she finally returned to Cedarville, Jane's health was much improved. But her brother, Weber, who was running the mills once owned by their father, had just suffered a nervous breakdown. Jane had to step in and take over the mills' operations and Weber's investments. His condition worsened until finally the family put him in a mental institution. Surprisingly, in the face of this challenge, Jane became physically stronger. While she assisted her brother's family, she also continued her father's practice of aiding others. She helped Rockford raise money for a telescope and a new library. In 1882, following in her father's footsteps, Jane was named to the college's board of trustees.

Despite her success with these enterprises and her improved physical health, Jane still suffered from depression. Haldeman recommended a trip to Europe. She wrote to a friend: "It seems quite essential for the establishment of my health and temper that I have a radical change. And so I have accepted the advice, given to every exhausted American—'go abroad.'"

Jane had doubts about the trip, even though she intended to comply with her doctor's advice. She wrote, "I quite feel as if I were not following the call of my genius when I propose to devote two years' time to travel in search of a good time." But she went ahead with her plans. Anna Addams and six friends went with her. On August 22, 1883, they left New York aboard the *Servia*. Although Jane began the trip wearing the awkward brace, she removed it during the trip and never wore it again.

Educated Americans often made trips to Europe to discover their roots and to absorb the culture. America was such a young country with so little history that travels in Europe were considered necessary for any well-rounded, worldly education. During the first two months of the tour, Jane and her companions visited the British Isles. Great Britain's Queen Victoria, who ruled over one-fourth of the world's land, held a special fascination for Americans. Jane was determined to get to know the ordinary people as well.

As was customary, Jane kept an account of all of her travels in a notebook. But one particular incident burned itself into her memory. One Saturday evening, her group joined a city tour of London. In the East End of the city, on Mile End Road, Jane witnessed the street vendors disposing of their last wares—mostly decaying fruits and vegetables. They had to get rid of the food because British law prevented Sunday sales, and it would not keep until Monday.

Ragged, pale-faced people thronged around two carts. With their few coins, they bid for whatever vegetable the peddler hawked. For a moment, from the bus, all Jane could see was hands grabbing for rotting food. Then one man detached himself from the group. "He had bidden in a cabbage, and when it struck his hand, he instantly sat down on the curb, tore it with his teeth, and hastily devoured it, unwashed and uncooked as it was."

Jane continued her tour of the museums, cathedrals, and art galleries of Holland, Germany, Austria, Italy, Greece, and France. She saw many other examples of poverty in the slums of these countries, but no place impressed itself upon her memory as much as the scene in London's East End. The experience added to her desire, first felt in childhood, to help the poor. The more she saw of the world, the more uncomfortable she became about her own life: "I am simply smothered and sickened with advantages. It is like eating a sweet dessert the first thing in the morning."

Jane despaired—she had finished college, toured Europe, and yet accomplished nothing of significance. She wrote to her friend Ellen: "I have been idle for two years because I had not enough vitality to be anything else. I have lost confidence in myself and have gained nothing and improved in nothing." After twenty-one months in Europe, Jane decided to return to Cedarville. She sailed from Liverpool, England, aboard the *Servia,* on May 30, 1885.

As soon as she got home, Jane went to help her sister Mary who had just given birth to another baby. Mary had been ill throughout the pregnancy. With three other young children at home and her husband working in another town, Mary could not cope. Jane stayed with her sister for several months.

In December, Anna Addams insisted that Jane join her in Baltimore, where George was taking courses at Johns Hopkins University. Her stepmother again forced Jane into a meaningless round of social activities. Whenever she could slip away, Jane visited a nursing home for elderly African American women and an orphanage that trained young African American girls for employment. Jane discovered that time she spent with Anna Addams playing a socialite exhausted her, but the days she spent visiting the nursing home and the orphanage were invigorating. These experiences confirmed her desire to help the poor, but she still had no idea how.

Jane spent the following summer in Cedarville, where she quickly became burdened with family problems again. Her brother Weber was back in the mental hospital, and Jane had to help his family. She feared that her life was destined to be that of an old-maid aunt who went wherever her family needed her most. When her sister Alice gave birth after twelve childless years of marriage, Jane uncomplainingly traveled to Kansas to help out.

However, in the back of her mind burned the desire to go back to Europe. Her friend Ellen Starr had told her how difficult it was to teach students at the Kirkland School about art without any actual examples of it to show them. From her first trip to Europe, Jane knew there were plenty of reproductions of famous paintings for sale in museums. When George dropped out of medical school in December 1887 and returned to Cedarville, Jane decided that he was perfectly capable of dealing with any future family crises. She was going abroad.

Accompanied

Ellen Gates Starr. *(Courtesy of University of Illinois at Chicago, University Library, Jane Addams Memorial Collection.)*

by Ellen Starr and Sarah Anderson, a teacher from Rockford, Jane left on December 14, 1887, for her second trip to Europe. This tour would mark a turning point in her life. She found that she could function independently of her family and that she enjoyed the company of other women her own age. Most importantly, it was on this trip that she finally understood the direction her life should take. She realized that there must be other young women like herself who had money and time but no purpose. She would provide them that purpose by finding a way to bring the rich young women and the poor together.

The three young women arrived in London a few days before Christmas and from there traveled to Paris. Jane went on to Munich, Germany, by herself. When she rejoined her friends in Rome, she received some sad news. Mary's youngest daughter, four-year-old little Mary, had died of whooping cough. Jane had been close to her niece. Her grief was so intense that she again became ill. Her friends continued their tour while Jane remained in bed for a month. During her enforced rest, Jane pondered the visit she had made to the Ulm Cathedral in Germany.

One of the things that impressed her most about the fourteenth-century structure, even more than the magnificent architecture, was the way the cathedral's many carvings, paintings, and stained-glass windows captured a wide variety of people. She remembered the place as a "cathedral of humanity dedicated to brotherhood, understanding, unity, and spiritual aspiration." Could she somehow build a modern cathedral of humanity?

In 1888, Jane was well enough to join her friends in

Jane in Europe in 1890, appearing confident and nearly regal. *(Courtesy of University of Illinois at Chicago, University Library, Jane Addams Memorial Collection.)*

Madrid, Spain, where they decided to attend a bullfight. Jane's friends left before the event ended because they could not stand the sight of the animals being killed. Jane, however, was strangely drawn to the pageantry of the occasion. She paid as much attention to the audience members' bright clothes and fans and the ladies wearing lace scarves over their heads and shoulders as she did to the bullfight itself.

When she rejoined her friends, they criticized her for having enjoyed such a bloody spectacle. As Jane thought about their accusations, she had a blinding flash of self-revelation. She realized that she had postponed doing anything about her dreams by continuing to travel. She later wrote in her journal: "I had fallen into the meanest type of self-deception in making myself believe that all this was in preparation for great things to come."

Jane decided that she needed to act. Tentatively, she spoke about her ideas to Ellen Starr. Jane proposed finding a house in a large city that had many needy people. They would equip the house and use it as a base from which to reach out to the poor. They would establish a "cathedral of humanity." To Jane's surprise and delight, Ellen understood her vision exactly. Having the support and encouragement of her best friend gave Jane the push she needed to start making her dreams a reality.

Jane needed a model for her plan. She soon found that there were several such houses in Great Britain. The country had been one of the first in Europe to go through the Industrial Revolution. Thousands of people had poured in from farms and villages to seek work in the factories. These poor and now landless families lived in tiny, dirty tenements. Some never got off the street. An entire generation had lived their whole lives without homes of their own. This led to an increase in crime, which led to the creation of the first modern police forces and the building of jails. There were other social concerns—disease, prostitution, and overburdened urban infrastructures.

Some in London and other cities had tried to do something about the problems brought on by industrialization. Jane visited the People's Palace, a large building that was a neighborhood center with meeting rooms, workshops, and clubrooms for the working poor. She was most impressed by Toynbee Hall, the world's first settlement house, or community center, established to confront poverty in a large city. In 1875, Arnold Toynbee, a student at Oxford University (and father of the modern historian of the same name), had moved into the heart of London to find a useful way to aid the poor. There he met Samuel Augustine Barnett, an Anglican priest, who believed in Christianity in action. Toynbee envisioned a settlement house as a place where a group of people could come to live in a poor section of the city. Living there, immersed in the problems, they could better understand the people around them and find practical ways to improve the situation. Toynbee, however, died at the age of thirty-two, before he could see his dream realized.

The Reverend Barnett carried on Toynbee's vision. He raised enough money to build a huge mansion in the middle of Whitechapel, one of London's worst slums. Fifteen young men, all recent university graduates, paid a small fee for room and board. When not working at their chosen occupations, they donated their time to the residents of Whitechapel.

Some of the services provided were lectures, practical classes, such as sewing and nursing, and even more advanced courses in chemistry, Greek, Latin, and

Shakespeare. They sponsored trips to art exhibits, concerts, and libraries and petitioned city officials to improve the area by cleaning the streets, opening more parks and libraries, and providing better schools.

As she toured Toynbee Hall, Jane realized that she had found her focus. She now had a goal. She wrote to her sister Alice: "It [Toynbee Hall] is free of 'professional doing good'. . . sincere and so productive of good results . . . that it seems perfectly ideal." For eight long years, since she finished school at Rockford, Jane had searched for a way to make a real impact on those who needed her help. She would not just knit bandages or visit hospitals once a week. She would change lives. She returned to the United States ready to put her plan into action.

Chapter Three

Building Hull House

The population of the United States more than tripled in the fifty years between 1840 and 1890, by which time there were nearly sixty-three million people living in the country. Many of the newcomers who had flooded into the "land of opportunity" were immigrants from Europe and Asia. As had happened earlier in England, new industries attracted people from rural areas into the expanding cities, where many sought work in the factories.

The reform movement in England had been motivated by the plight of the urban poor, and a similar situation now existed across the Atlantic in America. Jane Addams was not the first to take up the cause of the urban poor in the United States. What came to be called the Progressive movement was already gaining strength across the country. The early Progressives had been motivated by the fight against slavery. When the Civil War was over, many of the former abolitionists turned their attention to other pressing social causes.

Jane had followed her father's example and never officially joined a church. She had resisted baptism at Rockford because she felt it was being forced upon her. Still, she was a religious person and wanted to belong to a religious organization. Much of the strength of the reform movement came from churches and Jane admired the dedication to service she saw in church members. When she returned to the United States, she decided to be baptized into the Presbyterian Church in Cedarville. Although she did not accept all of the church's doctrine, by joining it she emphasized that her commitment to the poor was a religious act. From Cedarville she planned to move to bustling Chicago.

The illness of her sister Mary's son Stanley temporarily interrupted Jane's plans. Mary still grieved over the loss of her little daughter, and Jane felt obligated to help the sister who had cared for her when she was a child. As soon as Stanley's condition improved, though, Jane was on her way.

The city of Chicago had a population of nearly two million people by the time Jane arrived. Chicago had survived the great fire of 1871 and now railroads came from every direction to the second largest manufacturing center in the United States. Huge pens of animals waited to be slaughtered outside the great meatpacking plants. Over eighty percent of the population was made up of immigrants and their children.

In January 1889 Jane and Ellen Starr began to search for a neighborhood where they could implement their plan. Most of the immigrants were crowded together in

Poverty and disease were commonplace in Chicago's poorer neighborhoods. *(Courtesy of University of Illinois at Chicago, University Library, Jane Addams Memorial Collection.)*

dirty slums in Chicago's West Side. The first time she viewed this part of the city, Jane wrote: "The streets are inexpressibly dirty, the number of schools inadequate, sanitary legislation unenforced, the street lighting bad, the paving miserable . . . and the stables foul beyond description. Hundreds of houses are unconnected with the street sewer." Garbage was dumped directly into the Chicago River, polluting the drinking water and leading to periodic outbreaks of the dreaded typhoid fever.

Jane and Ellen rented rooms in a boarding house. They turned first to the churches and got offers of assistance from several prominent ministers. They also sought out the wealthier members of Chicago society. Although Jane knew that she wanted to model her experiment after Toynbee Hall, she had not developed all of the specifics.

Eventually, they decided their venture would have two purposes: to help those in need and to provide an outlet for the intelligence and skills of college-educated young women. By listening and talking to a variety of people, Jane began to formulate a specific plan. She knew that she needed a large house that had enough rooms for classes as well as rooms for other women like herself who would want to work on the project. She and Ellen began to look for a suitable building.

Touring Chicago's West Side, the two women saw street after street of the same kinds of "horrid little houses" Jane had first seen in Kilgrubbin. For five months they searched for a house throughout Chicago's Nineteenth Ward, home to thousands of immigrants from numerous countries. Following suggestions from architects, newspapermen, and city missionaries, they chose the area around Halstead Street because several immigrant neighborhoods were located nearby. As Jane traveled in a carriage up and down the street's thirty-two

Hull House as Jane first saw it. Streetcar tracks ran right in front of the building. *(Courtesy of University of Illinois at Chicago, University Library, Jane Addams Memorial Collection.)*

miles, she looked for a large building in the midst of the immigrant slums. Her quest ended one Sunday afternoon on Chicago's Halstead Street.

The first time she caught a glimpse of the two-story red brick mansion she knew that it was the one. The dirty structure needed work, but its white wooden pillars and broad porches appealed to Jane. But that night, as she described the house to Ellen Starr, Jane realized that she had not made a note of its exact location. After that, each time she went out in her carriage, she searched both sides of the street for the house, but she could not find it again. Halstead Street was the longest straight street in the world and it took several outings before Jane finally found the house again, on the corner of Halstead and Polk Streets.

Built in 1856 by a real estate speculator, Charles J. Hull, the house had escaped the Great Chicago Fire. Now a rental property sandwiched between a saloon and a funeral home, much of the building was already occupied. Another saloon and a furniture factory occupied most of the first floor while several families lived on the second floor.

In the neighborhood, there was a superstitious belief that the house was haunted. The people living on the second floor kept a pitcher of water on the stairs leading to the attic, believing ghosts were unable to pass through water. Helen Culver, who had inherited the property from Charles Hull, rented Jane all of the unoccupied rooms. Undisturbed by ghost stories, Jane moved into the house with Ellen and their housekeeper, thirty-year-old Mary Keyser.

They faced layers of soot and a variety of repairs, but hard work did not scare them away. The air reeked of rotting food, stagnant water, sewage, and coal dust. Garbage, filthy rags, and newspapers littered the streets that served as the playgrounds for the neighborhood's children. Here, Jane Addams established Hull House and began a lifetime of social reform and service to the poor.

Hull House was a way for Jane to help the poor by making use of the culture and knowledge of art, music, and history that she had acquired in college and during her travels abroad. Jane and Ellen balanced each other in this endeavor. Jane was the calm, businesslike partner while Ellen brought to the relationship her love of art and music, a deep religious faith, and a commitment to causes.

Ellen also had a wide circle of acquaintances in the Chicago area, thanks to her teaching position at the Kirkland School. These people helped to get Hull House started. When Jane and Ellen began, they were unaware that Hull House was not the first settlement house in the United States (that honor belonged to the Neighborhood Guild, established in New York City in 1886), but it soon became the most famous.

When Jane and Ellen chose to open Hull House in the midst of a neighborhood populated by immigrants from all corners of the world, they were confronted with the prejudices the various groups had toward one another. Jane planned to overcome these mostly ethnic and religious grudges by having Hull House open to persons of all races, creeds, and nationalities.

Before opening the doors, Jane had to get the house ready. She spent over $3,000 on repairs, and furnished the house with donated pieces and another $1,800 worth of furniture that she

Jane greeting visitors to Hull House. *(Courtesy of University of Illinois at Chicago, University Library, Jane Addams Memorial Collection.)*

The interior of Hull House, after renovations. Jane decorated the house so that it would have a welcoming feel to all who entered. *(Courtesy of University of Illinois at Chicago, University Library, Jane Addams Memorial Collection.)*

bought with her own money. Jane wanted her poor neigbors to have a beautiful, comfortable place to come to. She decorated the house with the art reproductions she had purchased on her second European trip, displayed her own silverware on a sideboard, and brought in other personal items as though she were setting up housekeeping for a family of her own. As news of their undertaking spread, offers of assistance poured in. Several newspapers and magazines published articles about the settlement. Wealthy Chicago residents, including Louise deKoven Bowen and Mary Rozet Smith contributed time, money, and advice. Another important benefactor was Hull House's owner, Helen Culver, who eventually donated the building and all of its adjoining property to Jane Addams.

People in the neighborhood were both curious and suspicious about what was happening at the big house. They were won over gradually, as they visited Hull House and witnessed its residents becoming involved in neighborhood affairs.

When it opened, Hull House had both female and male residents. All of them held full-time jobs, paid room and board, and gave their spare time to Hull House's activities. Two of the men who resided there were William Lyon Mackenzie King, who later became prime minister of Canada, and Gerard Swope, the future president of General Electric Company.

That these educated, middle-class professionals had chosen to live among them impressed the immigrants. Jane stated: "From the first it seemed understood that we were ready to perform the humblest neighborhood services. We were asked to wash the newborn babies and to prepare the dead for burial, to nurse the sick, and to 'mind the children.'"

One of the first official acts at Hull House was the opening of the nursery. Jane observed that mothers often locked their children in their apartment during the working day. Unable to afford childcare, desperate women left their children unsupervised for hours at a time. As a result, a number of tragedies had occurred: one child had been crippled after falling out of a third-floor window, another had been badly burned, while a third child had developed a curved spine from being tied all day to the leg of a kitchen table.

In the hot days of summer, many of the neighborhood children were locked out of their houses. Once they discovered the cool rooms at Hull House, they were loath to leave. The children quickly learned that they could always get a good meal at Hull House. For sixteen years, the Hull House nursery operated out of a cottage on a side street. Later, a building called the Children's Home was built specifically to house the nursery.

As Jane got to know the mothers of the children in the neighborhood, she realized the terrible stress that was put on women who had to work long hours and care for their families. One blustery March morning a woman was hanging out laundry on her rooftop as her little boy, nicknamed Goosie, ran around and from time to time handed her clothespins. Hurrying to finish her task, the mother did not see her son stumble and fall to the street below. The entire neighborhood gathered around as the grieving mother clasped the body of her little son. When Jane arrived, she asked what she could do to help. The mother asked Jane to give her the amount of money that she would have earned in wages the next day so that she could afford to stay home and hold the body of her dead son. She confessed to Jane, "Goosie was always asking me to [pick him up] and I never had any time." While he was alive she had been too busy, and now that he was dead she wanted only to give him the thing he had valued most—time alone with his mother.

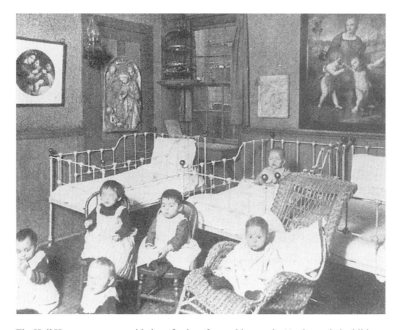

The Hull House nursery provided a safe place for working mothers to leave their children.
(Courtesy of University of Illinois at Chicago, University Library, Jane Addams Memorial Collection.)

Jenny Dow, a friend of Jane's from Chicago's wealthy North Side, volunteered to start a kindergarten. In the first month, she reached her maximum enrollment of twenty-four and had a waiting list of seventy.

Jane and her volunteers organized a variety of clubs for the older children. The girls enjoyed cooking and sewing classes, but the women had a harder time finding activities for the boys. Jenny Dow had brought Mary Rozet Smith with her to Hull House. Mary, who became Jane's lifelong best friend, accepted the challenge of entertaining the boys. She taught them to play pool and board games such as chess. She read them stories about

Jane's idea for a public playground was radical for its time. *(Courtesy of University of Illinois at Chicago, University Library, Jane Addams Memorial Collection.)*

heroes on the long, hot summer afternoons. Soon the boys were inspired to form a Young Heroes Club.

Though she was pleased by the results of their nursery, kindergarten, and afternoon clubs, Jane remembered her own carefree childhood days and longed to get the children outdoors. It would be too difficult to bring them all to the country, so Jane decided to bring the country to them. She discovered that a rich young man named William Kent was the owner of three-quarters of an acre of land next door to Hull House. Over a period of time, Jane convinced him to donate the land, tear down the old buildings on it, and continue to pay taxes on the property so that a play area could be developed. On May 1, 1892, Chicago's first public playground opened in the shadow of Hull House: "It was open to both children and youths . . . sand piles, swings, building blocks, and [a] giant slide [were] provided for the younger children, while the boys of adolescent age played handball and indoor baseball. An experienced kindergartner and a policeman supervised the playground."

The idea that Jane proposed was a radical one for the time. It was difficult to imagine that any businessman would agree to let land he was paying taxes on sit idle, all for the amusement of some poor children. But there was at this time a growing awareness of the concept of social responsibility. More and more people were interested in making the world a better place for everyone, not just the wealthy few.

Inspired by Hull House's example, public support for play areas and parks in the Chicago area grew. Daniel H. Burnham and the Olmstead brothers, architects and designers of the Chicago's World Fair in 1893, did the landscaping and architecture for all of the subsequent parks. In 1906, the movement had gained strength and organized into the Playground Association of America— with Jane Addams elected vice-president. The organization's first convention was held, appropriately enough, at a playground, so the delegates could see just how important it was for the children to have a place to play. Jane Addams was a pioneer in a movement to care not just for the body, but for the soul.

Chapter Four

Social Justice

Having provided an outdoor play area for the Nineteenth Ward's children, Jane turned to other problems facing the same girls and boys. Because she came from such a different background from her neighbors, it took her a while to understand their lives. Her first insight occurred at a Christmas party at Hull House. Everyone in the neighborhood, young and old, came to the party for which Jane and Ellen bought food, gifts, and candy with their own money. When Jane offered candy to a group of young girls, the children shrank back. Jane could not understand their aversion to candy until they told her "that they worked in a candy factory and could not bear the sight of it."

Jane learned that they sat close together at long tables, wrapping and packing caramels piece by piece for a few pennies per one thousand. They worked fourteen hours a day, eighty-two hours a week, from seven A.M. to nine P.M. Their only break was twenty minutes for lunch; they

Jane Addams hoped to put an end to the exploitation of children in factories such as the one pictured above. *(Courtesy of the Library of Congress.)*

received no supper break. This deeply shocked Jane. She decided to investigate further. That same winter, Jane heard another story from boys attending the clubs at Hull House. Three of them had been injured on a machine because the factory owner refused to buy an inexpensive guard to protect them. Another boy had been killed trying to operate the same machine. The owner took no action, saying only that the parents had signed papers agreeing to make no claims against the factory if their children were hurt.

Jane had not realized how much poor families depended on their children's jobs. Many of the adults could not find work, but their children could. Some of the worst abuses of children occurred in what were known as sweatshops. In Chicago's First Ward, factory workers cut cloth from patterns. Middlemen, called sweaters, contracted to get the jobs of stitching the cloth, making buttonholes, and putting on other finishing touches. Sweaters bid for these jobs at such cheap costs that the only way to make money was to give extremely low wages to the women they hired to do the sewing. The women received their scant salaries based upon the number of pieces completed. Consequently, even very young children assisted their mother with the work to complete more pieces. Middlemen crammed large numbers of women and children into dark, stuffy rooms. Jane described the situation: "An unscrupulous contractor regards no basement too dark, no stable loft too foul . . . no tenement room too small for his workroom."

At the time, it was illegal for any child under fourteen to work in a manufacturing establishment, factory, or workshop. Employers were supposed to keep records of the ages, addresses, and abilities of any children they employed and to be ready to provide these records to inspectors. The children were supposed to give a statement confirming that they had attended school until they were fourteen and could read and write in English, which had to be confirmed by an affidavit from their parents.

Florence Kelley, one of Hull House's earliest residents, was appointed the chief factory inspector for Illinois. When she realized how widely the law was being violated by the sweatshops, she asked for an investigation and was appointed to head that study. In 1894 she described some of the conditions that she found: "Many of the boys in these shops are buttonholers, and every little buttonholer is destined, sooner or later, to develop a curvature of the spine. Other boys run foot-power machines and the doom that awaits them is consumption of the lung or intestine."

The sight of very young children working ten hours a day, every day, for pennies an hour appalled Jane: "I remember a little girl of four who pulled at basting threads hour after hour, sitting on a stool at the feet of her . . . mother, a little bunch of human misery." In her report to the Illinois state legislature, Florence Kelley confirmed Jane's observation: "From the age of eighteen months few children able to sit in high chairs at tables were safe from being required to pull basting threads."

Factory owners depended on child labor because it was so cheap. If they had to reduce the number of hours children worked, or improve their working conditions, the owners would lose money. As the women of Hull

This boy is pulling basting threads from finished garments. Children were used for this work because of their small hands. *(Courtesy of the Library of Congress.)*

House continued to uncover these abuses, Jane was offered a bribe of $50,000 to stop the investigation. The toughest opposition came from glass manufacturers who claimed they simply could not make glass without child workers—they said that adults and even older children had hands too big and clumsy for the delicate work.

Jane could see the factory owners' point of view as well as that of parents who depended on their children's wages. But as always, her heart was with the children; she continued to gather information to try to fight abusive practices. As other people became aware of the problem, they too sought to learn more. One investigative reporter discovered that garments sent from the sweatshops to the leading Chicago department stores were often bringing disease with them. Largely because of unsanitary conditions, poor children were often sick with the highly infectious diseases typhoid and smallpox. Sick children in sweatshops sleeping, sweating, coughing, or sneezing could contaminate clothing. An unsuspecting customer who purchased one of these garments also bought smallpox or typhoid fever. For three months Jane spoke every night to any group that would listen—churches, unions, and clubs—to convince people of the need for a law to regulate child labor.

In March 1893 a bill was introduced in the Illinois state legislature that forbade children under the age of sixteen from starting to work before seven A.M. or working later than seven P.M. Children under fourteen had to stop working at six P.M. The maximum number of hours a child under sixteen could work was eight hours a day and forty hours per week. No child under fourteen, except newsboys, could work for anyone other than a parent. And no woman could be required to work more than eight hours a day or six days a week.

Although the bill, known as the Illinois Factory Act, passed on July 1, 1893, its opponents fought its implementation. In 1895 the law was repealed. But Hull House supporters, especially Florence Kelley, took comfort in the public attention they had brought to the problem of child labor. As Kelley said, "At least, the sweatshops are never going to be the same again."

While Jane and her associates pursued the problems related to children's working hours, a group of young female factory workers formed the Jane Club at Hull House. They were inspired by the recent failure of a strike at a shoe factory. The young women working in that factory had tried to use a work stoppage in order to obtain better working conditions and higher wages. But when the factory's management threatened to fire them all, the girls returned to work. They could not afford to lose their jobs. Management knew this, and used it to break the strike.

Hull House purchased and provided two furnished apartments on nearby Ewing Street. They guaranteed the first month's rent for the fifteen girls who moved in on May 1, 1891. After that, the club set up an emergency fund to collect contributions. The fund could then be used as support in case one of them lost her job for demanding improvements in working conditions. The Jane Club also offered a place where the girls could have friends visit and where they could practice housekeeping skills. Most of the girls had never taken care of a house or learned how to cook a meal—they had spent their lives at work, not at home where they might have observed and learned domestic tasks.

The Jane Club proved to be immensely popular and

Members of a Hull House youth club. *(Courtesy of University of Illinois at Chicago, University Library, Jane Addams Memorial Collection.)*

soon more space was needed. Jane sought donors. A friend of a Hull House trustee offered to contribute $20,000, and people were shocked when Jane refused the money. The man had a reputation for mistreating his own workers and Jane was determined that he would not assuage his guilt with cash. Eventually $15,000 came from a man named William Colvin. The Jane Club, a project dear to Jane Addams's heart because the idea came from people in the neighborhood, opened its new building in 1898. Within three years, the Club had fifty members who lived in the building's six apartments.

Though there was always much more to be done, Jane and her volunteers could see the positive impact they were making on their community. For a while, things seemed to be going very well—then the Pullman strike changed everything.

In the early 1800s, George M. Pullman, the manufacturer of the railroad sleeping cars, constructed a "model" town nine miles south of Chicago. He built it for the eighteen hundred people employed at his sleeping-car factory, who were required to live there. Pullman took pride in the town's attractive features—a library, a post office, a company store, parks, paved streets, a theater, a hotel, a church, and a school. What visitors could not see was that most of the apartments had no bathtubs; there was only one water faucet per five apartments. The model town helped give Pullman complete control over his workers. He not only controlled wages, he also set the cost of rent, water, gas, and groceries, which his workers had no choice but to purchase from him.

After the United States' financial panic of 1893, the company cut wages by thirty percent but made no reduction in rents. Many of the workers could not make ends meet on the lower wages. Class distinctions became more pronounced and bitterness developed between management and workers. As one employee complained, "We are born in a Pullman house, fed from a Pullman shop, taught in the Pullman school, catechized in the Pullman church, and when we die we will be buried in the Pullman cemetery and go to Pullman hell."

The American Railway Union, led by its president Eugene Debs, helped the Pullman workers to organize a grievance committee. Unions were a relatively new concept. There were few, if any, laws to protect workers. Just like the young women who formed the Jane Club, most workers were hesitant to try to unionize or strike for fear of losing their jobs and homes. So it took great courage for the three-member committee to appeal to Pullman and one of his vice-presidents, Thomas H. Wickes, on May 9, 1893. Although the two men refused to restore the previous salary level, they assured the committee members that there would be no action taken against them for having presented the grievance. But the very next day, the committee members lost their jobs. Debs led the call for a strike, and in the next few days fifty thousand railroad workers, including five thousand Pullman employees, responded. A new grievance committee was formed that demanded that the employees' case be heard within five days.

Jane Addams was one of six members appointed to a Citizens Arbitration Committee. She represented the group in its first talk with Pullman. Although Jane knew George Pullman personally—he had made a contribution to Hull House—she kept an open mind and tried to understand both sides. Pullman did not understand why Jane paid attention to the strikers' complaints. He believed he had every right to operate his business as he chose, and he refused all efforts to settle the disagreement.

When the committee was unable to settle the dispute, the American Railway Union struck in sympathy with

Union leader Eugene Debs with striking railroad workers. Early unions faced tremendous pressure from employers. *(Courtesy of Eugene V. Debs Foundation.)*

the Pullman workers. The *New York Times* called Eugene Debs, the union's leader, a "lawbreaker at large and enemy of the race." Railroad traffic in and out of Chicago was almost entirely shut down, creating a major problem for manufacturers, mine owners, and meatpackers. The Managers Association responded to the strike by bringing in temporary replacement workers (commonly called "scabs") from Canada to operate the trains. This resulted in clashes, often violent, between the strikers and their replacements. Eventually, even the mail delivery became affected, which gave the federal government a reason to intervene on the side of the manufacturers. On July 2, 1894, government officials arrested Debs on charges of conspiracy to obstruct the mail—a federal crime.

Riots broke out, and despite the protests of Chicago Mayor John Hopkins and Illinois Governor John Peter Altgeld, President Grover Cleveland sent federal troops to Chicago to quell the riots and keep mail delivery going. There was bloodshed, but the presence of the federal troops forced the strike to end. The strikers and their families had gambled and lost.

In the summer of 1894, Pullman reopened his factory after firing over one-quarter of his employees. He rehired the rest only after they signed contracts agreeing never to join a union. Attorney Clarence Darrow defended the union leader, Eugene Debs, in a case that established Darrow as an advocate for social justice. Although Jane had no involvement in the strike beyond that one meeting with Pullman, the conflict between workers and owners troubled her deeply. The bloodshed offended her pacifist

Illinois governor John P. Altgeld, a friend and supporter of Jane and her work at Hull House. *(Courtesy of Illinois State Historical Library.)*

religious beliefs, and the long-term effects of such violent confrontations worried her. Were things really getting better?

Jane's own family was directly affected by the strike. Her oldest sister Mary had been seriously ill for a long time with terminal cancer, and Jane had arranged for Mary to receive treatment at a hospital in Kenosha, Wisconsin. The height of the strike happened to coincide with Mary's condition worsening. As she neared death, the doctors sent for her family.

Jane traveled to Wisconsin on a private train car that was not involved in the strike, but Mary's husband and four children were unable to reach her bedside in time. Mary spent her last hours asking when her family was coming while Jane tried desperately to explain the embattled situation that kept them from her side. Mary died on July 6, 1894.

After her sister's death, Jane wrote an essay in which she compared George Pullman to William Shakespeare's King Lear. Jane pictured both men as kind-hearted dictators who believed that they knew what was best for others—Pullman for his workers and Lear for his daughters. The implication was that, in the end, Pullman would end up like Lear—unhappy and alone, too blinded by his convictions to see his mistakes. Jane was careful not to take a stand on the strike and did not mention Eugene Debs, but no newspaper or magazine would publish "A Modern King Lear" until 1912, eighteen years after the strike.

When Jane returned to Chicago after her sister's funeral, she brought Mary's eleven-year-old son Stanley with her. Mary had named Jane the guardian of her youngest child, who was not physically strong. He had lived at Hull House for only a few weeks before a typhoid epidemic broke out. Fearing for the sickly child's health, Jane sent him to a boarding school outside the city.

Walking through the neighborhood in the following weeks, Jane noticed scraps of white fabric stuck on many doors. Each tiny piece of white crepe indicated the death of a child. Feelings of guilt swept over Jane. She wrote in her diary: "I may well be ashamed that other delicate children who were torn from their families, not into boarding school but into eternity, had not long before driven me into effective action" against the poor health conditions. Jane could not reconcile herself to a world in which rich children could live but poor children would die.

Only fairly recently, the germ theory of disease had become widely accepted. In the 1860s, work done by Louis Pasteur in France had demonstrated that diseases did not arise spontaneously, as had previously been believed, but were instead the result of infection that spread through bacteria. This discovery slowly led to an increased awareness of the importance of sanitation. In the Nineteenth Ward, where Chicago's poorest people lived, sanitation was a luxury, not a fact of daily life. Stacks of rubbish spilled onto the broken pavement from huge wooden garbage boxes. Peddlers dumped unsold fruits and vegetables into alleys. Children played in streams of raw sewage. The stench from the stockyards and sewers filled the air. Women and children sorted rags in the city dump and carried them home to wash and sell, bringing germs with them. Flies, fleas, and rats—all carriers of disease—thrived in the muck and grime.

The Hull House Women's Club, a group of neighborhood women who met for lectures and discussions, began an investigation into the removal practices of the privately contracted garbage collectors in the Nineteenth Ward. By law, landlords were required to provide receptacles for trash and contractors were required to remove it. But corruption and carelessness meant the streets were always dirty. For three nights a week, in the heat of summer, the Women's Club searched for violations. That first summer they found and reported to the city health department 1,037 dangerous practices.

The next spring, when the city accepted new bids for garbage removal, Jane Addams personally submitted a bid for the Nineteenth Ward. Although the city claimed her bid was not valid, the mayor appointed Jane as garbage inspector for the ward at a salary of $1,000 per year. It was the only paying job Jane ever held.

Every morning Jane rose at six to follow the garbage collectors through the streets of the Nineteenth Ward. She was tough on violators. If garbage fell from a wagon, Jane made the collector pick it up. She pressured the removal contractor to double the number of garbage wagons on the street. If necessary, she used the courts to force landlords to provide enough collection boxes for garbage. Soon Jane could announce the good news that the Nineteenth Ward's lot had improved. At one time the area's death rate had been the third highest in Chicago and now it ranked seventh.

However, Jane could not continue the close monitoring of the garbage collectors and handle all of her other duties as well. She hired Amanda Johnson, who had done similar inspection work in other cities, to finish out the term of office and gave her the $1,000 salary. Although the cleanliness of the streets had improved, Jane knew this was just the beginning.

Chapter Five

Challenges and Growth

The lack of proper sewage disposal and other public health problems led to periodic typhoid fever outbreaks in the crowded city. No matter how much a mother might clean her own house, she could not protect her family from such things as raw sewage and improperly buried bodies that leaked germs into the drinking water supply. An epidemic of typhoid fever that swept through Chicago provided further incentive for people to take action about the lack of sanitation. During one epidemic, the Nineteenth Ward, which contained only 1/36 of the city's population, accounted for 1/6 of the deaths.

More progress in solving the ward's sanitation problems could not come, however, until corrupt politicians were removed from power. Jane twice tried to get rid of the Ward's Alderman, Johnny Powers, who had opposed Hull House activities. Along with Hull House residents and supporters, she backed another candidate, but Powers was a powerful politician. He served as chairman of

Jane Addams in 1889. *(Courtesy of University of Illinois at Chicago, University Library, Jane Addams Memorial Collection.)*

the Finance Committee of the Chicago City Council and used his financial influence to sway voters by doing little favors such as paying for a funeral, providing a job, bailing someone out of jail, or getting passes for the railroad. These gestures made voters believe he really cared about them.

Jane and the Hull House Men's Club, a group of men who lived in a dormitory on the Hull House property, got one of their own members, Frank Lawler, elected as an independent alderman. However, within only a few months, he accepted a bribe from Powers and switched his allegiance to the powerful politician. In 1896, the Hull House supporters ran William Gleeson, a forty-two-year-old Irish immigrant, as a candidate against Powers.

Although this attempt also failed, Powers's margin of victory was less than in previous elections. Encouraged, the Hull House supporters decided to put all of their energies into the 1898 campaign. Powers fought back in the newspapers, telling a reporter: "The trouble with Miss Addams is that she is just jealous of my charitable work in the ward . . . Hull House will be driven from the ward, and its leaders will be forced to shut up shop."

One newspaper, the *Chicago Chronicle,* and a group of Catholic priests in the Nineteenth Ward, joined Powers in his attacks. The priests claimed that the people at Hull House were against both Catholics and immigrants. To offset that accusation, Hull House sponsored as a candidate for alderman an Irish Catholic, Simeon Armstrong, who had lived in the ward for thirty years.

Despite Armstrong's background, Powers won by an even greater margin than usual, receiving eighty percent of the vote. After his victory he bragged: "I may not be the sort of man the reformers like, but I am what my people like, and neither Hull House nor all the reformers in town can turn them against me." He was right; he held office for another twenty-four years.

Jane Addams did not waste her energy on impossible tasks. She moved on to another challenge. The conflict with Powers convinced her that real reform had to come from the state and national levels. She began to speak to a larger audience through a series of magazine articles and lecture tours she took throughout the United States. She collected the speeches into her first book, *Democracy and Social Ethics,* which was published in 1902.

Jane continued to work on other troubling situations in the Nineteenth Ward. Although the ward's many immigrants brought artistic skills from their native countries to the United States, their American-born children had no appreciation for their parents' abilities and no understanding of the relationship between those skills and the goods that were produced in the factories. The Industrial Revolution had made such skills outdated, as machines took over the weaving of cloth, woodworking, and numerous other crafts. Jane wanted to preserve the craftsmen's art and skills before they were lost forever.

One day, as Jane walked through the neighborhood, she stopped to speak to an old Italian woman who was using a stick spindle to spin thread. The woman explained she was trying to make enough thread to knit a pair of stockings for her goddaughter.

Watching the woman use an ancient skill gave Jane the idea of establishing a place where older immigrants could demonstrate their talents and teach them to a new generation. Most immigrant children took pride in being Americans and shunned their parents' old-world ways. Jane wanted this to change. The valuable skills of basket-making, cabinet-making, spinning, weaving, sewing, embroidery, carving, pottery making, and metal work should not be lost.

At first Jane had only one room at Hull House available for the demonstrations, but their popularity led to the development of an exhibition place called the Labor Museum. As the older immigrants taught their crafts, the children developed an appreciation for their cultural backgrounds. Young people learned about the relationship between raw materials and the finished product. They could understand the stages of development that went from handicrafts to the machines they operated in the factories. Of all the activities at Hull House, the Labor Museum pleased Jane the most. Its success led a Hull House trustee, Julius Rosenwald, to devote millions of dollars to fund the Rosenwald Industrial Museum in Chicago.

Jane Addams's work at Hull House changed her own life as much as, and perhaps even more than, it changed the lives of the people in the community. Between her two trips to Europe in 1883 and 1887, Jane had read *War and Peace* by Leo Tolstoy. The great Russian writer regretted the way the Russian upper class mistreated the common laborers. He attempted to make up for these wrongs by changing the way he lived. Tolstoy, who was from a wealthy family and owned huge tracts of land, began to live, dress, and eat like a peasant. He worked in the fields and used his spare time to make boots with his own hands. Jane admired Tolstoy's courage in living out his beliefs. This idea appealed to her and other Americans who realized they spent too much idle time amidst an abundance of goods.

In 1896, after recovering from a bout of typhoid fever, Jane took her first vacation in seven years. She visited Tolstoy at his home in Yasnaya Polyana (a village in central Russia), but the meeting did not go as she hoped. Tolstoy criticized her clothing, specifically the fashionably puffy sleeves on her dress. He later told her: "There was enough stuff on one arm to make a frock for a little girl." He believed her fancy dress put a barrier between her and the poor people with whom she worked.

Tolstoy encouraged Jane to do her own chores at Hull House. That night, as Jane and his other guests ate an elaborate meal, Tolstoy ate only porridge and black bread.

When she returned to the United States, Jane could not get Tolstoy's ideas out of her mind. At Hull House one day she felt so guilty she spent the entire afternoon baking bread. She had learned the skill in her childhood because her father had required each of his daughters to produce a perfectly baked loaf of bread on their twelfth birthdays. John Addams, too, had believed in the importance of self-sufficiency.

Jane's politics were also shaped by her Hull House experience. In the spring of 1898, the Spanish-American War broke out because of Spain's policies in Cuba. The war was over in three months, but Jane Addams did not think the United States should interfere in the internal

Jane and Hull House were devoted to helping the children of Chicago's poorest neighborhoods. *(Courtesy of the Library of Congress.)*

affairs of other nations. She became a committed supporter of peace, saying: "Peace was not merely an absence of war but the nurture of human life." Jane's time at Hull House had convinced her that what was most important in the world was taking care of people, not destroying them in senseless wars.

After speaking at the Thirteenth Universal Peace Conference in Boston in 1904, Jane collected her speeches in a 1907 publication, *Newer Ideals of Peace*. She believed that people could reorganize their priorities away from war. She wrote: "We care less each day for heroism connected with warfare and destruction and constantly

admire more that which pertains to labor and the nourishing of human life." She saw this nourishment as an
appropriate and valuable substitute for war and said: "I
do not imagine if the human race once discovered the
adventure to be found in the nourishing of human life . . .
they would look back with much regret."

Her horizons were expanding beyond the Nineteenth
Ward of Chicago, but Jane still spent more time dealing
with problems in the Hull House than promoting world
peace. One constant concern was the high rate of juvenile delinquency. Even though most children worked,
they were generally expected to turn over their wages to
their parents. If they wanted to buy some candy or see a
movie at the new and popular five-cent nickelodeons,
they often resorted to stealing and pickpocketing.

Because the arrival of a fire truck or a patrol wagon
was exciting, kids sometimes purposely did things just to
get a response from the police and firemen. Trains and
railroad tracks were frequent targets. Boys built fires
along the railroad tracks, broke signal lights, and threw
stones at moving train windows. They turned switches,
which sometimes caused streetcars to run off their tracks,
and cut telegraph wires. They stole barrels of linseed oil
from the railroad and set them on fire so they could
watch the fire engines rush down the street.

Thousands of juveniles were arrested and tried every
year. Jane Addams charged that "practically the whole
machinery of the grand jury and the criminal courts is
operated for the benefit of youths between thirteen and
twenty-five." Because there was no juvenile court, young

people were tried as adults and sent to adult prisons. Prisons were unregulated, dangerous places that, if the youth survived, would almost surely turn him into a life-long criminal. One of Jane's friends at Hull House, Julia Lathrop, was especially concerned that juvenile offenders, who often committed minor offenses, were tried as adults. Julia had been appointed to the Illinois Board of Charities in 1893 and helped to organize a Juvenile Court. She served as the first president of the Juvenile Court Committee. Her goal was to rehabilitate juvenile offenders rather than punish them. The committee established the first juvenile probation system in the nation to keep a watchful eye on young offenders and to support their rehabilitation.

Judge Julian Mack, who backed the new system, explained this change in how the courts handled juvenile offenders: "It was the conception that a child that broke the law was to be dealt with by the state as a wise parent would deal with a wayward child." The first probation officer, Alzina P. Stevens, lived at Hull House. At the age of thirteen, Stevens had worked in a textile mill in Maine. She lost her right index finger in an accident at the factory. The missing finger constantly reminded her of the need to take better care of children. Stevens saw the probation officer position as a way for her to reach out to juveniles.

Another Hull House supporter, Louise deKoven Bowen, joined Julia Lathrop in setting up the juvenile court and probation system. Bowen facilitated the necessary legislation to provide salaries for probation workers and a detention home so that youths would not have to go to adult jails. Jane later used much of the material collected by the Juvenile Court Committee in her book *Spirit of Youth and the City Streets,* published in 1909.

Jane's passionate views, genuine concern for the welfare of others, and tireless work on behalf of the poor, made her one of America's most admired women. She had gained widespread respect through her work, her lecture tours, and her writings. But an event outside of her control damaged her reputation and made her a more controversial figure.

The assassination of President William McKinley occurred in September 1901 when Leon Czolgosz, an anarchist, shot the president in the stomach at a public reception in Buffalo, New York. McKinley lingered for eight days before he died, on September 14.

This assassination reminded many people of the Haymarket Square tragedy sixteen years earlier. On May 3, 1886, workers at the McCormick Reaper Works had gone on strike to obtain an eight-hour workday. When the police tried to intervene, violence erupted, killing one man and injuring another. Some anarchists (people who advocate for the dissolution of governments and other power structures that create unfair hierarchies) planned a rally for the workers to protest at Haymarket Square, a site near Halstead Street.

On the night of May 4, the rally drew to a close around ten o'clock and people started to go home. Fewer than two hundred remained on the square when the police arrived and demanded the workers leave immediately.

Suddenly a bomb exploded, followed by gunshots. The explosion killed one policeman, Mathias J. Degan, immediately. Six others died later as a result of their injuries. Panicked by the bomb, the police opened fire on the crowd. Sixty more policemen were injured in the crossfire. No one knew the number of workers killed or injured because their family and friends hurried them away.

Police response to the incident at Haymarket Square was immediate and fierce. They arrested all known anarchists the next day. Of the thirty-eight named in the criminal indictments, only eight men stood trial. No one could ever identify the bomb thrower, but those eight men were convicted of making speeches that caused the people to riot. Judge Joseph E. Gary gave the death sentence to seven of the accused and a fifteen-year prison sentence to the eighth one.

Four of the accused were hanged on November 11, 1887. One committed suicide in jail and the sentences of two were later changed to life in prison. The man who had escaped the death penalty remained in prison, even though authorities could prove no case against him. When John P. Altgeld took office as governor of Illinois, he reviewed the three cases personally. He found no evidence of guilt. Although he told a friend "If I do it, I will be a dead man politically," he granted the men full pardons on June 26, 1893. But it was too late. Public opinion had solidified against the men. Anarchists became reviled figures, associated with violence and destruction.

Because Leon Czolgosz was identified as an anarchist, rumors about the possibility of another Haymarket incident spread. Many of Chicago's immigrants who held progressive political views were arrested. One of the arrested was a Russian Jewish man named Abraham Isaak, who published *Free Society,* a newspaper that often took issue with the government. The arrest of the middle-aged father of two angered those who believed him to be unfairly targeted for exercising his right to free speech. When family and friends were forbidden to see Isaak, they went to Jane for help. She, in turn, appealed to her friend Mayor Carter Harrison to allow her to visit Isaak, who was being held in solitary confinement in a dirty cell beneath city hall. She wanted to be able to assure his family and friends of his well-being.

Despite public opposition, Mayor Harrison allowed Jane to visit Isaak—but he ordered that sixteen policemen accompany her. Soon after her visit, Isaak was released because there was no evidence that he had participated in any crime. By this time, however, many Chicagoans feared Isaak and the radical views he espoused. As well, he became the focus of the long-simmering fear and hatred many felt toward immigrants and poor people. Jane was considered guilty by association. She received a flood of hate mail and people threw rocks at Hull House. Suddenly, negative opinion of Jane was rampant, and public support of her work began to fade.

Though she understood that not everyone would support her, Jane was still hurt by the way her reputation was besmirched. A year after the Isaak debacle, John P. Altgeld—long-time supporter of Jane and Hull House

Over the years, Hull House grew from one house to multiple buildings. *(Courtesy of University of Illinois at Chicago, University Library, Jane Addams Memorial Collection.)*

and, by this time, former Illinois governor—passed away. His body lay in state at Chicago's Public Library, where thousands of the people he had helped filed past his casket to pay their last respects. He and Jane had worked together on child labor laws and on setting working hours for women. Though he had been loved and appreciated by the people he served, his belief that relief for the poor was a function of the government had angered factory owners and other business leaders. He had become unpopular within the wealthy and middle class. Inevitably, he was branded an anarchist for pardoning the three men charged with inciting the Haymarket Riot.

Jane Addams was one of the few people who rose to speak at Altgeld's funeral service. Another was Clarence Darrow, the lawyer who had defended Eugene Debs after the Pullman strike. Both Addams and Darrow praised the former governor's life and work. After voicing her support for Altgeld, Jane and Hull House lost the support of several prominent businessmen, just as some of her friends had warned might happen. But Jane gained another important supporter, the former leader of the Rough Riders during the Spanish-American War, Theodore Roosevelt, who had become president of the United States after McKinley's death. While he was governor of New York, Roosevelt had tried to improve slum conditions in New York City and had used Hull House as his model. With his public support for her work, and the undeniable effect Hull House was having on its neighborhood, Jane Addams's reputation was slowly restored. By 1907, Hull House consisted of thirteen connected buildings covering an entire city block.

Chapter Six

The Progressives

As Hull House's reputation and influence grew, Jane Addams was slowly drawn onto a larger stage. Her investigations into juvenile delinquency had let her see the connection between school truancy and delinquency. In July 1905 she became a member of the Chicago Board of Education. She took on this job at a time when the Board and the Teachers' Federation were in conflict over teacher salaries and the teachers' right to have input into the schools' curriculum.

When the Teachers' Federation discovered that five public utility companies were not paying any taxes, it filed a lawsuit to force the board to tax the corporations. They won the suit and brought $250,000 in new revenue to the board—but the board did not use the money to increase the teachers' salaries. The Teachers' Federation then sued the Board. This case was under appeal when Mayor Edward F. Dunne appointed Jane to the board.

Jane became chairperson of the board's School Management Committee that had responsibility for teacher promotion, curriculum, supplies, and salaries. She hoped to bring to the Chicago schools a sense of a higher purpose. She said: "Our schools must give the children better and truer standards for judging life. Life does not ask whether a man can read or write, so much as it asks whether he can use whatever faculties have been given him." She envisioned a school system that prepared students to succeed in life.

Usually Jane could get parties in conflict to compromise, but she had no luck with the school board and the teachers. Before long, she had made everyone angry as she tried not to favor one group over another. The teachers accused her of not taking a stand in order not to offend any Hull House contributors. Though Jane was trying to use her neutral stance to bring both sides together, she came across as indecisive and wishy-washy.

When Mayor Dunne lost the next election, the incoming administration asked many of the Board of Education members to resign. Jane was not among those asked to leave, and the ousted members expected her to speak up in their defense. When she failed to do so, her former supporters were upset and charged that she had sold them out. Jane summarized the situation: "My efforts were looked upon as compromising and unworthy of both parties." Despite the criticism, Chicago schools felt her influence for many years after she served on the board, and many schools throughout the United States have been named for her.

Jane's term ended after four years when the new

mayor refused to reappoint her. This would not be the only time her efforts to influence events on a larger stage would have an unhappy ending. She was learning that it was much easier to effect change on the local level than the global level—but she was also learning that it was very difficult to say no when people asked her for help.

In 1909 Hull House celebrated its twentieth birthday. Jane began writing her autobiography, which described those busy years. She dictated her story to a secretary who typed on a continuous roll of paper. At first, Jane did not try to put the events in any order but described them as she thought of them. Later she and the secretary cut apart the long sheet and used straight pins to fasten pieces together in chronological order.

The book, called *Twenty Years at Hull House,* was published in 1910 and contained memories from her childhood and youth as well. Jane wanted to reach as many people as possible, so she allowed *Ladies' Home Journal,* a national magazine with a large number of readers, to publish short selections from the book.

In addition to her writing, Jane continued to advocate for better working conditions. On September 29, 1910, a sixteen-year-old girl quit her job as a seamstress at Hart, Schaffner, & Marx in Chicago because the company cut her wages a quarter of a cent per garment. Nineteen other girls decided to walk out with her. Within three weeks, the strike had spread throughout the garment industry, shutting it down.

Jane Addams and two others were asked to try to resolve the issues of working conditions and wages.

When her committee received the suggested agreement worked out between the strikers' leaders and the company, it contained a section that denied workers collective bargaining power. Collective bargaining, which meant workers could band together to negotiate with their employer, would provide the opportunity for employees and employers to try to reach agreement on wages, hours, and working conditions—before a strike occurred.

Jane refused to sign off on the agreement because it denied collective bargaining. She told the garment workers' leader, Sidney Hillman: "Your own people will never agree." She was right. All 90,000 workers quit and the strike continued for weeks. Hart, Schaffner, & Marx finally agreed to remove the clause. This was a radical move. Both the president of the company, Harry Hart, and Sidney Hillman later became Jane's good friends.

Years later, Jane wrote an article about an incident that occurred at Hull House at the time of the strike. The article described the superstitious belief once held by many of the Nineteenth Ward residents that Hull House concealed a devil baby. People of all backgrounds came to Hull House begging Jane to let them see the demon child. There were many different rumors about this evil infant's appearance and the reason for its existence.

One version of the story claimed that a devoutly Catholic woman had gotten pregnant. Her husband, an atheist, resented her devotion to her religion. One night he supposedly stripped a holy picture off the wall. He said that he would rather have the devil in his house than such religious foolishness. The story held that his wish was granted—his wife delivered the devil baby, complete with cloven hoofs, pointed ears, and a small tail. Another version of the infant's origin described a man who bemoaned having six daughters and no sons. When his wife became pregnant again, he said that he would rather have the devil himself than another daughter.

Though there were many different variations on the story, they all had a similar conclusion. In each case, the father took the devil baby to Hull House. Never one to turn away a child, the residents had supposedly accepted the strange child, wrapped it in a blanket, and presented it to a priest for baptism. As the priest reached for the baby, his hands touched an empty blanket. He looked across the church and saw the child running across the backs of the pews to avoid touching the holy water.

This story spread quickly; at times hundreds of people lined the street outside Hull House, hoping for a glimpse of the little devil. The telephone rang constantly with requests from individuals and groups outside the Nineteenth Ward to arrange tours. After several weeks, the newspapers picked up the story. Reporters came to watch the crowds more than to look for the alleged devil baby.

Jane tried to understand the unusual situation. As she studied the crowds, she noticed that most of the people lined up to see the devil baby were old women who might have immigrated years before but had not become accustomed to American ways. She talked to many of them and realized they were looking for some evidence that what they had believed all their lives still held true in their new country. To them, the story of the devil baby was an affirmation that wrongdoing would be justly punished, that blasphemous people would reap what they sowed. After a while, the story of the demon baby wore thin and the crowds dispersed. But it emphasized for Jane the difference between the generations in the immigrant population and led her to search for new ways to bridge that gap.

Once again, Jane's work at Hull House led toward a grander stage. She knew that the problems she saw in her neighborhood would never be changed until the underlying causes were changed. This conviction led inevitably to politics and the question of suffrage (voting rights). Jane thought everyone deserved a voice in the political process. Her interest in woman's suffrage extended back to her childhood. Her father's Quaker beliefs sought justice for all. He had supported early feminists such as Lucretia Mott and Elizabeth Cady Stanton, organizers of the first convention for women's rights, held in Seneca Fall, New York in 1848. After the Civil War, John Addams also approved of the work of the famous suffragist Susan B. Anthony, who founded the National American Woman Suffrage Association (NAWSA).

Jane Addams first stayed in the background of the woman's suffrage movement, although she had quietly supported its efforts since her college days. She did not participate in a NAWSA meeting until 1906, when she was in her mid-forties. Jane's first convention also happened to be Ms. Anthony's last; the older activist died not long after. In 1907 Jane led an unsuccessful campaign to gain women the right to vote in city elections in Chicago.

Suffragettes marching in the early 1900s. *(Courtesy of the Library of Congress.)*

In 1911 Jane and Catherine Waugh McCulloch managed a state campaign for woman's suffrage in Illinois. They hired a train to carry three hundred women to the state capital of Springfield, where they presented their case in a one-and-a-half-hour session with a state legislative committee. They succeeded in getting the bill for woman's suffrage placed on the legislative calendar, but it was defeated when it came up for vote. Later that same year, Jane was elected NAWSA vice-president, a position she held for two years.

NAWSA held its 1912 convention in Philadelphia. Because that city is fairly close to Washington, D.C.,

Jane led a delegation of one thousand women to testify about women's voting rights before the U.S. House Judiciary Committee, as women had done for the past forty-two sessions of Congress. The committee members listened and even asked questions. The committee promised to carry the women's report to the full House of Representatives, but did not follow through on the promise. The measure did not come up for a vote until the following year, when it lost in both the House and the Senate.

Unlike other suffragists, Jane Addams did not see woman's suffrage as only a natural extension of the Declaration of Independence. She also claimed that the government had taken over many jobs once handled by women, such as concerns for health and safety. "Most of the departments in a modern city can be traced to women's traditional role," she pointed out. If women did not participate in government, they would be "losing what they have always had."

In her opinion, women had more sympathy and appreciation for suffering than men did. Women should become involved in solving America's industrial problems as an extension of their job to protect children. She argued: "Women do not wish to do the work of men nor take over men's affairs. They simply want . . . to take care of those affairs which naturally and historically belong to women, but which are constantly being overlooked and slighted by our political institutions."

Jane charged that women could no longer just do the simple tasks of keeping their own house clean or feeding their children because society's problems had now intruded upon the individual home:

> Women who live in the country sweep their own dooryards and may either feed the refuse of the table to a flock of chickens or allow it innocently to decay in the open air and sunshine. In a crowded city quarter, however, if the street is not cleaned by the city authorities no amount of private sweeping will keep the tenement free from grime; if the garbage is not properly collected and destroyed a tenement house mother may see her children sicken and die of diseases from which she alone is powerless to shield them . . . if woman would keep on with her old business of caring for her house and rearing her children she will have to have some conscience in regard to public affairs lying quite outside of her immediate household.

She argued that women's votes would reflect their experience and skills and that this would improve communities.

Jane spoke out about suffrage from any platform she could find. She gave a speech in a New York vaudeville theater and made a film with NAWSA president Anna Howard Shaw. Newsreels shown at theaters before the main feature included this silent film. In June 1912 Jane led a group of women to the Republican National Convention in Chicago. They were allowed only seven minutes to present their case for including a woman's suf-

A cartoon depicting Jane Addams bringing the problems of the poor, the elderly, and the children to President Roosevelt. *(Courtesy of the* Boston Journal.*)*

frage plank in the Republican platform. The attempt failed. However, other important decisions that occurred during the convention had a direct influence on Jane's activities for the remainder of the year.

After the assassination of President William McKinley, Teddy Roosevelt served as President from 1901 to 1909. He did not run for reelection in 1908 but his hand-picked successor, William Howard Taft, was the Republican presidential nominee. In 1912, Roosevelt, who was deeply disappointed that Taft had not carried forward his progressive agenda, decided that he wanted the party's nomination again. Taft, though, refused to step down.

When he lost the nomination to Taft by a vote of 561-107, Roosevelt and his supporters walked out of the Republican Convention. They formed the Progressive Party and developed a platform of advocating social and industrial justice. Because of Jane Addams's experience, Roosevelt wanted her in the Progressive Party. Jane had her own agenda—including woman's suffrage. She thought the Progressive Party could accomplish that goal.

The newly formed political party seemed to bring together the many separate causes for which Jane and others at Hull House had worked during the past twenty years. At the party's August 1912 political convention in Chicago, Jane helped to draft a national program for all of those social concerns. The party's platform included minimum safety and health standards for various occupations, a prohibition on child labor, minimum wage standards for women, and an eight-hour workday for women and young people. Jane stated: "The Progressive Platform contains all the things I have been fighting for for more than a decade." She also believed that the time was right to introduce, on a broader scale, the idea of equal voting rights for all citizens regardless of race, color, or gender.

Although Jane supported most of the party's platform, she had some differences with Roosevelt. His demand that two new battleships be built each year and insistence on the fortification of the Panama Canal conflicted with

Jane's own pacifism. But her biggest disagreement with Roosevelt was over his refusal to seat Southern black delegates at the party's convention. He allowed only white delegates from the Deep South to be seated despite protests from Jane and other members of the National Association for the Advancement of Colored People (NAACP), which Jane had helped to found in 1909.

Jane disagreed with Roosevelt on these specific issues but still backed his candidacy for president. She even seconded his nomination at the party's convention, believing he offered the possibility of social reform in many areas. She told the delegates: "A great party has pledged itself to the protection of children, to the care of the aged, to the relief of overworked girls, to the safeguarding of burdened men."

After Roosevelt was nominated, a reporter asked him how he felt. The nominee replied, "Strong as a bull moose." The enthusiastic crowd broke into cheers and waved flags while a brass band played loudly. One delegate from Texas climbed up to the first balcony of the coliseum and kissed the head of a bull moose that had been placed there for decoration. After Roosevelt's comment and the Texan's kiss, the Progressive Party earned the nickname "Bull Moosers."

After the convention, Jane campaigned across the United States in support of Roosevelt and the Progressive Party platform. She traveled thousands of miles, often giving as many as three speeches in one day. She confidently shared the Progressive Party's optimistic belief that with the right laws, society could solve its social

Jane campaigned for the Progressive Party and woman's suffrage. *(Courtesy of the Swarthmore College Peace Collection.)*

issues. She received such enthusiastic support everywhere she spoke that she started to believe the Bull Moosers might actually win.

On the night before the election, she later recalled: "At that moment we believed that we were witnessing a new pioneering of the human spirit." When people questioned whether it was appropriate for her to be involved in party politics, she declared: "I never doubted for a moment that my place was inside, where there was a chance to help on such a program as this one."

Despite her critics, Jane's popularity soared. As another campaign worker commented: "Wherever I went I heard nothing but talk of Jane Addams, I suppose other political speakers had been out there, but you never would have guessed it from what people had to say." Jane's efforts could not carry the party to victory, however. Roosevelt and the incumbent, Republican President Taft, lost the election to Democrat Woodrow Wilson.

Though Jane was disappointed when Roosevelt lost, she believed the campaign had at least brought wider publicity to the need for social reforms. Since President Wilson backed some of the reform agenda when he took office and also worked to keep the United States out of World War I when it began in August of 1914, Jane supported him for reelection in 1916.

The next eighteen months brought victories for woman's suffrage in several states, including Illinois. Some people even encouraged Jane to consider a political career, but she refused. Whatever she did in the political arena was always in support of a cause, not for personal ambition. She had supported Roosevelt because she believed he shared her philosophy of social reform. If she had run for political office, Jane would not have been able to devote herself totally to the causes she favored.

Chapter Seven

Work for Peace

World War I, referred to at the time simply as "the war" or the Great War, had a devastating impact on much of the world. Resulting from decades of tension in Europe, the war pitted the Central Powers (Germany, Austria-Hungary, and Turkey) against the Allies (Belgium, Russia, France, Great Britain, and later Italy). The German plan was to open the war with an unprecedented sweep east across Belgium and France. They aimed to reach the English Channel in just a few weeks, thus becoming the *de facto* rulers of all of Europe. But the plan, which the German military had been developing for years, did not work out as intended. The Belgian troops put up a remarkable and brave fight against the far superior German and Austrian forces, slowing their advance and giving the French and British time to rush in troops. The Germans responded to the Belgian resistance by burning villages and shooting hundreds of civilians.

This brutality only strengthened the resistance. Great

Historians estimate that over seven million soldiers were killed in World War I. *(Courtesy of U.S. Military History Institute, Pennsylvania.)*

Britain entered the war to protect the Belgians and a French victory at the Battle of the Marne stopped the German advance. Before the winter snows began, a series of trenches stretched from the English Channel to the border of Switzerland. The two sides took refuge in the trenches, which were sometimes dug only a few hundred yards apart. For four years, the armies attacked and counterattacked with poison gas, machine guns, long-range artillery, and tanks. Casualties mounted at a horrific rate.

Despite the war, people throughout the world continued to work for peace. To Jane Addams, war was always wrong. It went against everything she believed in—

sympathy, negotiation, logical thought, and nonviolence. Even though the United States had not yet entered the war, feelings in America ran high, mostly against the Germans. Jane's pacifist stand was not popular. Theodore Roosevelt, the former Progressive Party candidate for whom she had so tirelessly campaigned, exclaimed: "Jane Addams—don't talk to me about Jane Addams! I have always thought a lot of her, but . . . she's all wrong about peace."

Though Jane had little desire to be a political figure, she could not ignore the war. She was convinced that the United States could not make life for its own citizens better by fighting a foreign war. She could not keep silent about her beliefs—even though they were unpopular.

On January 10, 1915, at the New Willard Hotel in Washington, D.C., Jane, along with three thousand representatives from many women's groups, organized the Women's Peace Party. The women, who elected Jane chair of their newly formed organization, had widespread experience in effecting change on such issues as clean drinking water, hot school lunches, and safe playgrounds. Now they turned their attention to world politics.

The preamble to their Peace Platform stated: "We, women of the United States, assembled in behalf of World Peace . . . do hereby band ourselves together to demand that war be abolished. . . . As women, we are particularly charged with the future of childhood and with the care of the helpless and the unfortunate. . . . We demand that women be given a share in deciding between war and peace in all the courts of high debate—

Jane (second from left) and others demonstrating for peace. *(Courtesy of the Library of Congress.)*

within the home, the school, the church, the industrial order and the state." The Women's Peace Party quickly grew to forty thousand members. Before the United States entered World War I, the party became the American branch of the International Congress of Women.

Under President Wilson's leadership, the United States maintained its neutrality. In April, despite growing pro-war sentiment in America, Jane and forty other women left the United States for the International Conference of Women in The Hague, Netherlands. The eleven hundred women gathered at this meeting came from twelve nations, some at war and others neutral.

The delegates felt that "women must show that we can retain our solidarity and that we are able to maintain a mutual friendship." The International Congress asked

Jane Addams to head their group. The delegates voted to try to get the warring nations to come to a neutral conference and enter mediation to end the war.

The women decided to carry their resolution to both warring and neutral countries. One committee, composed of Chrystal Macmillan, Rosika Schwimmer, Cor Ramondt-Hirschmann, and Emily Balch, visited the neutral nations. Jane Addams, Aletha Jacobs, Dr. Alice Hamilton, and a Dutch woman, Frau van Wulfften Palthe, visited those at war. They saw the ravages of war—bombed buildings, wounded soldiers, and starving people.

During their tour of the various countries, the women discussed ways to solve international problems without resorting to violence. They received varying responses to their ideas. In London they visited with Prime Minister Asquith, but the British were committed to the war. Austria approved the idea for a conference of neutral nations. German Foreign Minister Jagow said: "Germany would not be unfriendly to calling a conference of neutrals, but it would be doubtful if practical results would come from such a conference."

While Jane and her group talked to the warring countries, the committee visiting the neutral nations tried to get one of them to call the conference and agree to host it. No one was willing to assume such a responsibility, but a few indicated they would participate if the United States took the lead. At the conclusion of their travels, the two women's committees had planned to meet and compare notes in Amsterdam, Holland. However, Jane Addams felt that it was more important for her to go home and talk to President Wilson about calling a conference. She skipped the Amsterdam meeting.

Few observers believed that the international women's conference had solved anything, but the more optimistic among them felt they might have set the stage for future negotiations. By contrast, former President Teddy Roosevelt criticized the plan for mediation: "Pacifists are cowards, and your scheme is both silly and base," he said. Most people were just amused at the idea that women thought they could end a war. Jane appealed to President Wilson to initiate the mediation but he refused. Meanwhile, the casualties numbered ten to twenty thousand each day.

On May 17, 1915, German submarines sank a British ship, the *Lusitania,* as it sailed for Liverpool, England. One hundred twenty-eight Americans were among the 1,195 people who lost their lives. This action ended any real hope for the continued neutrality of the United States. As news of the deaths spread, enraged Americans spoke out against Germany. In the public's opinion, not to be actively opposed to the Germans was to be in support of them.

On July 9, 1915, Jane spoke at Carnegie Hall in New York about her European visit. Over three thousand people listened as she said that she found it difficult to make general statements about the war when her mind was so filled with images of specific individuals and events. She admitted that she had talked mostly to civilians as she traveled through the warring nations. Though people differed about the preferred method, they all agreed on the best possible outcome: an end to the war. People in the fighting countries did not speak out openly against the war because they wanted to support their militaries. But, Jane said, "Generally speaking, we heard it everywhere—that this was an old man's war; that the young men who were dying, the young men who were doing the fighting, were not the men who believed in the war." She talked about the strength of character it took for patriotic young men to question the war. In one case, several soldiers had committed suicide rather than kill another human being. As she spoke about the bloodshed and the fighting, she made a comment that she would later have reason to regret.

Jane had talked to soldiers from different countries who told her they relied on drugs or alcohol to give them the courage they needed to make a bayonet charge, "not because of any cowardice on their part," she insisted, "but because of their general loathing of killing." Jane had also heard from hospital nurses who reported that "delirious soldiers are again and again possessed by the same hallucination that they are in the act of pulling their bayonets out of the bodies of the men they have killed." When Jane repeated these examples in her speech, she meant to show her audience how difficult war was. Although she drew enthusiastic applause at Carnegie Hall, the next day headlines read: "Troops Drink-Crazed, says Miss Addams."

With her remarks, Jane Addams had unintentionally denied the idealistic notion that soldiers fight and die from a sense of duty and for the love of their country. By suggesting that some soldiers found war unpleasant or that they regretted their actions, she was undercutting the common belief that soldiers lived without fear. Although she had been talking about the European soldiers she had interviewed, American newspapers, many of which wanted the United States to enter the war, claimed she had dishonored all soldiers. She had no way of knowing how men felt in battle, they said, because she was neither a man nor a soldier.

Richard Harding Davis, a popular writer, wrote a letter to the editor of the *New York Times*. He criticized Jane's remarks at length, claiming she had belittled America's military. Similar editorials appeared in newspapers throughout the United States: "Jane Addams is a silly, vain, impertinent old maid, who may have done good charity work at Hull House, Chicago, but is now meddling with matters far beyond her capacity," was a typical sentiment. Lost in the wave of responses was the main point Jane had made at Carnegie Hall: "Every nation sincerely believes it is fighting for self-protection, for righteousness. . . . Each will hold out to the end of its strength unless some neutral power offers effective intervention. . . . America must lead the fight for peace and disarmament."

Bundles of letters, mostly critical, poured into Hull House. Most of her friends remained quiet and did not rise to her defense. Jane did not back down, but the attacks distressed her deeply.

In 1915, Hungarian pacifist Rosika Schwimmer visited the United States on a speaking tour. She read in the

A wounded soldier in World War I, receiving treatment on the battlefield. *(Courtesy of the U.S. Army Military History Institute, Pennsylvania.)*

newspapers that Henry Ford, manufacturer of the first automobiles, had said he would give half of his fortune to end the war even one day earlier, thus sparing the lives of at least ten thousand men. Schwimmer went to Detroit to speak to Ford. He was overwhelmed by her sincere enthusiasm and offered to sponsor several hundred Americans on a peace mission to Europe. He felt strongly about the war and wanted to do something to end it but had not been sure what to do. Based upon Schwimmer's recommendation, Ford decided to charter a ship to take the American delegation to Stockholm, Sweden, for a meeting to try to bring about a peaceful settlement. The slogan of the mission was "Out of the trenches never to go back."

Ford shared his ideas with Jane Addams. While she appreciated his enthusiasm, she worried that he lacked a solid, workable plan. She thought the whole project had been thrown together too hurriedly. Ford had some trouble clearly articulating the goals of his peace missions, and he and his "peace ship" quickly became a favorite target of newspaper writers and cartoonists. Despite her doubts about the trip, Jane felt compelled to join him. Her friends discouraged her, fearing that she would bring even more criticism to herself and to Hull House.

The *Oscar II* was set to leave New York on December 4, 1915. On December 1, Jane became ill from pneumonia and was taken to the Presbyterian Hospital in Chicago. The ship sailed without her. Jane's recovery was slow, and she went to California to recuperate. When she returned to Chicago, she became sick again. This time her doctor diagnosed tuberculosis of the kidneys. After having one kidney removed, Jane followed her doctor's orders to rest quietly. The newspapers accused her of pretending to be sick so that she could avoid the public humiliation of Ford's folly. Jane endured this criticism as stoically as ever.

On April 6, 1917, the United States finally declared war on Germany and entered the fighting on the side of the Allies. Public opinion was by this point overwhelmingly in favor of war. Even those who had initially opposed joining the fight were now prepared to stand squarely behind American troops. The peace movement was largely abandoned. Jane turned her attention to aiding the war's victims, especially children.

The United States government had been sending supplies of food and medicine to Europe since 1914, and Jane made an appeal to have the relief efforts increased. The establishment of the Department of Food Administration, headed by Herbert Hoover, pleased Jane, especially when Hoover showed that his attitude matched her own: "The situation [starvation] is more than war, it is a problem of humanity."

She volunteered to help in the efforts to get Americans to grow more food on uncultivated land while at the same time consuming less so the surplus could be sent to alleviate hunger in Europe. Wartime food for most Europeans consisted of heavy black bread, cabbage, and turnips, and dirty water ususally washed the meal down.

Jane traveled across the United States appealing to women to help conserve food: "In this great undertaking women may bear a valiant part if they but stretch their minds to comprehend what it means in this world crisis to produce food more abundantly and to conserve it with wisdom." She convinced people to participate in wheatless Wednesdays and meatless Mondays. Her book *Peace and Bread in Time of War,* not published until 1922, detailed this work. When Americans abstained from wheat on Wednesdays and meat on Mondays, they were able to reduce domestic consumption of these foods by fifteen percent. The plan had a strong psychological benefit as well, since Americans at home could feel that they were making sacrifices, even small ones, for the men at the front.

In November 1918, Germany surrendered and all of the warring nations signed an armistice, or declaration of peace. President Wilson traveled to Paris in the spring for a peace conference, taking with him his Fourteen Points plan. Many of the points represented goals developed by women at the first conference of the Women's International League for Peace and Freedom. A new point was the establishment of a League of Nations.

At the peace conference, decisions were made that seemed to take advantage of the defeated enemy rather than show them generosity or display the type of wisdom that could help avoid another war in the future. Wilson gave in on some of the fourteen points so that he could achieve the establishment of the League of Nations. The final terms of the armistice were harsh and one-sided in their punishment of Germany and Austria. Wilson returned to the United States, hoping the League of Nations would become a forum where nations could settle disputes peacefully. But his own country rejected membership in the organization, as well as participation in a proposed World Court.

Jane Addams and her colleagues were disappointed that Wilson had yielded on so many of the fourteen points. The International Congress of Women issued a statement saying: "The International Congress of Women expresses its deep regret that the terms of peace prepared at Versailles should so seriously violate the principles upon which alone a just and lasting peace can be secured." The women believed the Treaty of Versailles would create more hostility between nations and lead to future wars. Later events proved them right.

In June 1919, the American Friends Service Committee, a Quaker organization that worked for peace, sent Jane Addams, Mary Rozet Smith, and Dr. Alice Hamilton to Europe to assess the effects of the war on the people. Jane described some starving children she saw in northern France—little boys stripped to their waists waiting for a doctor to examine them for tuberculosis. Jane wrote: "Our first impression was of a line of moving skeletons: their little shoulder blades stuck straight out, the vertebrae were all perfectly distinct as were their ribs, and their long arms hung limply at their sides." The three women faced similar scenes wherever they went.

Some Quakers traveling with them brought a "love offering" valued at $30,000. (A love offering, in the Quaker tradition, is a gift given to others with no expectation of anything in return.) From the United States Food Administration they had purchased thirty-five tons of condensed milk, seventeen tons of sugar, and other foods. They planned to distribute these foods in Germany, even though the amounts represented only a small percentage of what was needed. But many Americans were already complaining about the food restrictions in the United States. To ask for more money to buy food for Germans, even German children, met with public resistance. Once again, Jane was faced with the realization that caring for others was not always an easy thing to do. Before Jane returned to Hull House, she made a personal pilgrimage. John Linn, Jane's oldest nephew and the son of her deceased sister Mary, had been killed at Argonne in northern France three weeks before the war ended. John, a forty-seven-year-old Episcopalian minister, had been exempt from the draft because of poor eyesight. But he became a chaplain with an army artillery unit. The day he died he was giving out chocolate candy to the men in his unit.

While inspecting conditions in northern France for the Red Cross, Jane searched for her nephew's grave. Somehow, among row after row of hundreds of little white crosses, she found it. Jane had been especially close to John, who was only twelve years her junior. His birthday and Jane's were three days apart. In letters he had written to Jane, he had said that he would never return to the United States: "I shall probably be killed, but if I am not I shall not come back. There will be too much to do over here that is worth while, and I should not like the thought of having come to Europe only for uselessness." Like his famous aunt, John Linn believed it was a person's moral obligation to care for and try to better the lives of others. Vowing that her trip to Europe would not be useless, Jane returned to the United States determined to continue her work.

Chapter Eight

Most-Admired Woman

The end of World War I brought many changes to the United States. Jane was delighted at the passage of the Nineteenth Amendment, which finally extended the right to vote to women, and applauded the establishment of the League of Nations, although she was disappointed that her own country refused to join the League. She returned home to dedicate herself to the more immediate problems in the Hull House neighborhood.

When America joined the war, many of the soldiers about to be sent overseas had quickly married their girlfriends. A good number of them had fathered a child before leaving, and it was not uncommon for families to have trouble adjusting after the men returned home. The soldier was trying to return to family life after the horrors of war, his wife was trying to readjust to having a husband after coping alone for so long, and his children often resented the presence of this stranger they were told was their father. Crime increased as unemployment soared. Wartime manufacturing quotas were drastically reduced just as the labor pool was swelling with returning soldiers. Many men were surprised to find women doing jobs that men had typically done before the war. Then another global tragedy struck. Influenza followed the troops home and quickly spread across the nation. Young mothers seemed to suffer worst from the often-fatal disease. Hull House workers tried to respond to the needs of their neighboring communities, but there were not nearly enough people or resources. At one time the almost universal respect for Jane Addams could have brought forth additional help. But now she was shunned for her pacifist views and her attempts to help the German people. Hull House, once a beacon of goodwill and good works, was forgotten.

While World War I was still raging, the Russian government had been overthrown. There had been two revolutions in Russia and by the end of 1917 the Communists had seized power. Now there were deep fears in Europe and the United States that Communism would spread throughout the world. Although there were few Communists in the United States, the horrible war, the fierce and sometimes ugly debate over the League of Nations, and the influenza epidemic, had left many citizens fearful and nervous. The Communist (a.k.a. "Red") threat was another source of stress that could be used by politicians seeking to gain favor. A Red Scare ensued, reaching its peak in the United States in 1919 and 1920. During this time any suggestion of reform was viewed with suspicion.

Thousands of foreign-born citizens, especially those

from Russia, were arrested, jailed, and deported for dissenting political views. Inevitably, many innocent people were caught up in the hysteria. The least criticism of the United States government was suspect. Having long worked with the immigrant communities at Hull House, Jane Addams did not think she had any choice but to speak out against the arrests and deportations. She called for an end to unfair and discriminatory policies. She argued that the people were being denied one of the very freedoms upon which America was founded—the right to free speech.

The press pounced on Jane again. The more conservative newspapers particularly took pleasure in such headlines as "Jane Addams Favors Reds." One Reserve Officer Training Corps publication charged that she was "the most dangerous woman in the country." Jane's name headed a list of sixty-two that the War Department watched for signs of disloyalty. The existence of the list itself was then called into question—its opponents argued that if Jane Addams was on it, it would have to include "everybody who during the past twenty years has tried to do anything for his fellow men."

Although the majority of the criticism that Jane faced came from only a small percentage of people, widespread newspaper coverage caused other Americans to wonder if the accusations were true. Reporters combined facts with half-truths and outright lies to connect Addams to Communism. Intricate charts, supposedly linking certain persons and organizations to some clandestine Communist conspiracy, began to circulate. Hull House was labeled a hotbed of radicalism. Jane pretended that such attacks did not bother her, but they did.

The Daughters of the American Revolution (DAR) cancelled her membership, claiming she was unpatriotic. Jane responded: "I supposed at the time that [membership] had been for life, but it was apparently only for good behavior." Large numbers of American Legion members would not forgive her wartime involvement in the Women's International League for Peace and Freedom. Jane did not back down, quipping: "You know I am really getting old. I find it not as easy to love my enemies as it used to be."

Some of Jane's friends and supporters advised her to file lawsuits to stop the slander. When she refused, they gave a huge dinner in her honor at the Furniture Mart, the largest floor space in Chicago. Fifteen hundred people attended the January 1927 event. Even more were turned away because they had not made reservations in time. Telegrams and letters of support poured in from all over the world, including a message of praise from President Calvin Coolidge.

Governor Alfred Smith of New York sent a telegram that read: "In honoring Jane Addams we honor the idealism of American womanhood." Jane responded to the praise with her usual modesty: "In a way I am humiliated by what you say, for I know myself to be a very simple person, not at all sure that I am right, most of the time not right."

But all this praise could not stop the cancellation of her lecture tours and other public appearances. As one newspaper opined: "She has lost something from the shine of her halo." As a result, Jane's income dropped dramatically.

Maude Royden, a British doctor, came to the United States for a lecture tour. She summarized the change in public opinion about Jane Addams that had occurred since her last visit:

> In 1912 I learned that it was unsafe to mention Jane Addams' name in a public speech unless you were prepared for an interruption, because mere reference to her provoked such a storm of applause. . . . After World War I, I realized with a shock how complete was the eclipse of her fans—her popularity had swiftly and completely vanished. How well I remember when I spoke in America in 1922 and 1923, what silence greeted the name of Jane Addams. The few faithful who tried to applaud only made the silence more depressing.

Though she put on a brave public face, her loss of popularity in America led Jane to spend more and more time abroad, although her official residence was still Hull House. In January 1923, Jane, now sixty-two, began a nine-month-long trip around the world. She focused her efforts on the Women's International League for Peace and Freedom. By the time she returned home, the United States was enjoying prosperous economic times. With that prosperity came a resurgence of the charity that had been so absent during and right after the war.

The Great Depression only made Hull House's services more important. *(Courtesy of University of Illinois at Chicago, University Library, Jane Addams Memorial Collection.)*

Louise Bowen donated seventy-two acres and ten buildings located in Waukegan, Illinois to Hull House. The plan was to establish the Bowen Country Club, where people associated with Hull House could go for fun and relaxation. Children fortunate enough to spend a week at the Club often experienced their first trip outside the city and enjoyed fresh air as they played outdoors.

By the middle of the 1920s, scattered and unexplained areas of unemployment threatened to burst the economic bubble. Then, in 1929, life in the United States changed drastically. A wave of selling on the New York Stock Exchange panicked investors. By the end of the day of

October 29, 1929, the stock market had crashed—trading losses totaled $23 billion. The Great Depression had begun.

As unemployment spread, families had no money to buy food and children were soon malnourished. People could not pay their rents; eviction notices on doors became commonplace. When banks could not recover loans they had to close. Hundreds of Chicagoans lost their life savings when the city's largest trust company failed. During this same year, Hull House marked its fortieth birthday, and public attention was brought to all that Jane Addams had done to help the poor. In 1930, at the age of seventy and suffering from health problems, Jane published *The Second Twenty Years at Hull House.*

Jane was popular again. She received several awards in 1931. *Good Housekeeping,* a prominent women's magazine, named Jane first among "the twelve greatest living women of America." A panel of men named her one of the six most outstanding Americans—and the only woman in the group. The alumnae of Bryn Mawr College, a respected women's college in Pennsylvania, presented her the $5,000 M. Carey Thomas prize for her contribution to American living. That same year Jane published *The Excellent Becomes the Permanent,* a collection of eulogies and tributes she had presented at funerals. She dedicated the book to her good friend, Dr. Alice Hamilton, who had cared for Jane through many illnesses. The dedication read: "To Alice Hamilton, whose wisdom and courage have never failed me when we have walked together in the very borderland between life and death."

Jane Addams (right) worked her entire life to make America and the world a better place.
(Courtesy of University of Illinois at Chicago, University Library, Jane Addams Memorial Collection.)

The year she turned seventy-one, the Nobel Prize Committee announced that Jane was a co-winner of the 1931 Nobel Peace Prize—the first woman ever to win the prestigious prize. She shared the award with Dr. Nicholas Murray Butler, longtime president of Columbia University, who was noted for his work with the Carnegie Endowment for International Peace. Some of Jane's friends resented her having to share the peace award with Dr. Butler because he had supported the United States' entry into World War I.

The award was to be presented in Oslo, Norway, on December 10. Jane, though, was in Johns Hopkins Hospital in Baltimore, Maryland, recovering from lung tumor surgery and a bad reaction to the anesthetic, and could not travel. Hoffman Philip, United States Minister to Norway, accepted the award on her behalf.

In his presentation speech, Halvadan Koht, a professor of history at the University of Oslo and a member of the Nobel Committee, said:

> In honoring Jane Addams, we also pay tribute to the work which women can do for peace . . . among nations. . . . Wherever women have organized, they have always included the cause of peace in their program. And Jane Addams combines all the best feminine qualities which will help us to develop peace on earth. . . . Little by little, through no attempt to draw attention by her work but simply through the patient self-sacrifice and quiet ardor which she devoted to it, she won an eminent place in

Even as awards and accolades piled up, Jane never abandoned her work at Hull House.
(Courtesy of University of Illinois at Chicago, University Library, Jane Addams Memorial Collection.)

the love and esteem of her people. . . . When the need became more pressing than ever, she inspired American women to work for peace on an international level. . . . Sometimes her views were at odds with public opinion both at home and abroad. But she never gave in.

Jane's share of the Nobel Prize money was $16,480. She gave $12,000 of it to the Women's International League for Peace and Freedom.

The Great Depression had a devastating effect on the country. Many blamed President Herbert Hoover for not doing more to alleviate the suffering. Because of her background in social work, both the Republican and the Democratic parties asked Jane to give her views to their platform committees as they prepared for the crucial 1932 elections. In the November election, Jane cast her vote for Hoover because she admired the work he had done to feed Europe's starving people after World War I. But Americans overwhelmingly wanted a change. Franklin Delano Roosevelt won a landslide victory because he offered citizens the hope for a better future.

At his inauguration the new president reminded Americans that they had overcome problems in the past: "In every dark hour of our national life a leadership of frankness and vigor has met with the understanding and support of the people themselves which is essential to victory. . . . Let me assert my firm belief that the only thing we have to fear is fear itself."

Roosevelt named Frances Perkins, a former Hull House resident, as his Secretary of Labor. Perkins was the first woman to hold a cabinet-level position. Jane Addams was a welcome advisor to both Perkins and the president. The labor secretary recognized Jane's special skills and knowledge, saying: "Jane Addams really invented social work and social welfare as a department of life in the United States."

The president and Perkins developed several measures to bring relief to Americans. The biggest item was the creation of a Social Security Administration to provide the third leg of a retirement plan that they said should include social security, individual savings, and company pensions.

Jane wholeheartedly supported the New Deal. She wrote to a friend: "It is really a wonderful time in which to live in spite of much suffering due to unemployment which still exists." It was an especially wonderful time for Jane Addams. Most of the criticism she had endured since World War I now turned to praise. She found herself a national hero. Jane and the First Lady, Eleanor Roosevelt, became good friends. They shared many of the same ideas. Mrs. Roosevelt would in future years inherit Jane's mantle as America's most-respected woman.

In 1935 Jane Addams received the American Education Award for her "willingness to learn from life [while teaching] tolerance and peaceful community living, first at home and then in the world at large." In February she went to Washington, D.C. to receive the award in a ceremony broadcast on radio throughout the world.

On May 2, Jane was back in Washington at the Willard Hotel for the twentieth anniversary celebration of the Women's International League for Peace and Freedom. Her poor health was obvious, but she participated in the evening's activities, which became more of a tribute to her than to the organization. Eleanor Roosevelt told Jane: "It is for being yourself that I thank you tonight. When the day comes when difficulties are faced and settled without resorting . . . to war, . . . we shall look back in this country upon the leadership you have given us, Miss Addams, and be grateful for having had you live with us."

The next day, in honor of Jane's approaching seventy-fifth birthday, a worldwide radio broadcast was scheduled. Speakers from all of the world's major cities offered praise for Jane Addams. Josephine Roche, Assistant Secretary of the United States Treasury, introduced Jane to the international audience. From the NBC station in Washington, Jane picked up her prepared speech, laid it down, and spoke without notes from her heart: "We don't expect to change human nature but we do expect to change human behavior." Despite the obstacles she had faced, Jane never stopped believing a better world was possible.

Jane returned home to Chicago, her health failing. She attended several meetings, her last one with the Cook County Commissioners on May 10. Five days later, she complained of a severe pain in her left side. Her doctor believed she had an intestinal blockage that required surgery. She was taken to Passavant Hospital for surgery on May 17 and placed as the only patient on the ninth floor.

When they operated the next morning, doctors found the blockage that was causing the pain, but they also found inoperable cancer.

After receiving the news, Jane remained in good spirits as she fought for her life over the next three days. She even joked with her friend Dr. Alice Hamilton, who kept a watch at Jane's bedside: "When I was a child, I had an old doctor friend who told me that the hardest thing in the world to kill is an old woman. He seems to have been right."

On May 20, Jane's temperature rose to 107.6°F, and she went into a coma. But her weak heart kept pumping until 6:18 P.M. on May 21, 1935, when she finally died. Mourning family, friends, and Hull House residents filled her hospital room and the halls of the ninth floor.

Over the next days the world remembered and honored Jane Addams. Resting in a plain, light gray casket on a bed of tulips, her body lay in state at Bowen Hall of Hull House from two in the afternoon until eleven the following morning. The Hull House Women's Club, the Hull House Dramatic Club, and former members of the Boys' Club served as an honor guard while children from various Hull House clubs acted as ushers.

Thousands of mourners—ordinary people, important businessmen, and politicians—passed by her casket at the rate of six thousand per hour. Dressed in their best clothes out of respect for "Miss Addams," almost twenty-five thousand paid tribute. For the funeral her body was moved to the Hull House terrace. Police closed Halstead Street to all traffic except streetcars. Shops and even the saloons up and down the street's thirty-two miles bore purple drapes of mourning on their doors and windows.

At 2:30 P.M. on Thursday, May 23, 1935, the funeral service began. People filled the streets around Hull House and climbed onto rooftops and fire escapes to get a better view. The next morning her body was transported to the Twelfth Street Railroad Station to begin the trip back to Cedarville. In that village, all of the businesses closed before the train's arrival.

Church bells tolled as the hearse made its way through

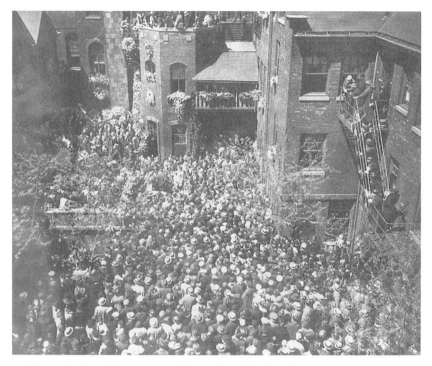

Thousands of people came to pay tribute to Jane at her funeral. *(Courtesy of University of Illinois at Chicago, University Library, Jane Addams Memorial Collection.)*

the town. Jane Addams was buried next to her parents and eight of her siblings in the little cemetery on the hill near her childhood home. At the graveside, under the Norway pines planted by her father, a group of children sang "America the Beautiful." Her tombstone reflected the two accomplishments of which she was most proud: "Jane Addams of Hull House and the Women's International League for Peace and Freedom."

Expressions of admiration and sympathy poured in from all over the world. Illinois governor Henry Horner said, "I think of her as the evening star, drawing the imagination of man through the clouds to the knowledge of a light that cannot fail." Perhaps the best tribute came from Walter Lippman, a nationally syndicated columnist:

> She had compassion without condescension. She had pity without retreat into vulgarity. She had infinite sympathy for common things without forgetfulness of those that are uncommon. That, I think, is why those who have known her say that she was not only good, but great. For this blend of sympathy with distinction, of common humanity with a noble style is recognizable by those who have eyes to see it as the occasional but authentic issue of the mystic promise of American democracy.

Many years removed from the emotion surrounding her death, historians have wrestled with determining Jane Addams's impact on social justice and world peace. During her lifetime, which spanned from the Civil War to the New Deal, she won some of her battles and lost many others. She was called both a saint and a villain. She never seemed to seek fame or greatness for herself. Instead she focused on helping those less fortunate. A wise and compassionate woman, she worked hard to put her beliefs into action.

Today, on the University of Chicago campus, two of the original buildings house the Jane Addams Hull House Museum. The museum stands as an internationally recognized symbol of social reform and justice, two of the necessary conditions for true and lasting peace.

Timeline

1860   Laura Jane Addams is born on September 6, to John Huy Addams and Sarah Weber Addams in Cedarville, Illinois.

1863   Sarah Addams dies on January 14.

1865   Abraham Lincoln assassinated on April 14.

1867   John Addams marries second wife, Anna Haldeman.

1875   Jane's oldest sister Mary marries Rev. John M. Linn.

1877   Jane enrolls at Rockford Seminary.

1881   Completes course of study at Rockford; President James A. Garfield, shot by assassin on July 2, dies on September 19; John Huy Addams, Jane's father, dies at age fifty-nine; in October, Jane enrolls in Woman's Medical College of Pennsylvania in Philadelphia.

1882   Receives bachelor of arts degree from Rockford College for Women; Jane's stepbrother/brother-in-law, Dr. Harry Haldeman, performs surgery on her spine; Rockford College for Women names Jane to its Board of Trustees.

1883   Jane sails for Europe, where she remains for two years.

1885   Returns to America.

1886   Haymarket Square riot occurs in Chicago, Illinois.

1887   Jane makes second trip to Europe.

1888   Visits Toynbee Hall in London seeking model for settlement house.

1889	Along with Ellen Starr begins search for a settlement house in Chicago; Jane and Ellen move into Hull House.
1891	Jane Club opens at Hull House; Jane appointed garbage inspector in Chicago's Nineteenth Ward.
1892	With businessman William Kent, establishes Chicago's first public playground, near Hull House.
1893	Chicago's World Fair opens; Hull House residents and supporters attack sweatshops in attempt to end child labor; Illinois Factory Act passes July 1; Pullman strike shuts down railroads.
1896	Jane visits Leo Tolstoy in Russia; Hull House residents and supporters oppose Nineteenth Ward boss, Johnny Powers; Labor Museum opens at Hull House.
1898	Spanish-American War begins.
1901	Assassination of President William McKinley by anarchist.
1902	Jane publishes *Democracy and Social Ethics.*
1905	Appointed to Chicago Board of Education.
1907	Jane publishes *Newer Ideals of Peace.*
1909	Publishes *The Spirit of Youth and the City Streets;* Hull House celebrates twentieth birthday; Jane helps to found the National Association for the Advancement of Colored People (NAACP).
1910	Jane publishes *Twenty Years at Hull House;* helps settle garment workers strike; "Devil baby" story sweeps Nineteenth Ward.
1911	Jane launches statewide campaign in Illinois for woman's suffrage; elected vice-president, National American Woman Suffrage Association.
1912	Leads 1,000 women to Washington, D.C. to testify about woman's suffrage; publishes *A Modern King Lear;* joins new Progressive Party when Teddy Roosevelt leaves GOP; seconds nomination of Teddy Roosevelt for president of the United States at Progressive Party's national convention.

1914   World War I begins in Europe.

1915   Jane helps form and is elected chair of Women's Peace Party in United States; presides over Women's International League for Peace and Freedom at The Hague, the Netherlands.

1917   Opposes America's entry into World War I.

1918   Joins Herbert Hoover's Food Administration to feed war victims.

1919   Leads International Congress of Women in protest of Treaty of Versailles.

1920   Incites public wrath by defending alleged communists and anarchists; Nineteenth Amendment establishes women's right to vote.

1922   Jane publishes *Peace and Bread in Time of War,* a record of her relief work during World War I.

1923   Begins nine-month around-the-world tour.

1927   Daughters of the American Revolution cancels Jane's membership in that organization; large dinner in Chicago honors Jane.

1929   The Great Depression begins.

1930   Jane publishes *The Second Twenty Years at Hull House.*

1931   Receives the Nobel Peace Prize.

1932   Publishes *The Excellent Becomes the Permanent.*

1933   Franklin Delano Roosevelt's New Deal begins; Twenty-first Amendment repeals prohibition.

1935   Jane wins American Education Award; addresses world by radio; dies of cancer in Chicago on May 21 at age seventy-four.

Glossary

advocate A person, in some instances a lawyer, who pleads another's cause.

alderman A member of a city council, representing a particular district or ward.

anarchist A person who advocates the dissolution of government.

apprentice A person learning a trade or skill.

arbitration The settlement of a dispute by a neutral party.

aspiration Strong desire or ambition.

atheist A person who believes there is no God.

authentic Real, genuine.

aversion Strong dislike.

blockade A shutting off of a port or region to prevent supplies moving in or out.

catalyst An event that causes something else to happen.

catechism The teaching, especially of religion, through questions and answers.

conception Idea.

condescension Dealing with others as though they are lower in worth or position.

consumption An old-fashioned term for the disease tuberculosis, or TB.

convulsions Seizures, spasms.

delirious Showing extreme mental excitement and confusion.

disarmament Reduction of armed forces and weapons as set forth by a treaty.

elusive Hard to keep clearly in mind.

eulogy A speech of remembrance, usually given at a funeral.

eviction Forcing a person from a house or apartment because of failure to pay rent.

forum A place where matters can be discussed openly.

feminists People who advocate equal political, economic, and social rights for both sexes.

grievance Complaint against a real or imagined wrong.

hallucination Seeing or hearing things that are not really there.

humiliated The act of being shamed.

impertinent Not showing proper respect.

incentive Something that makes a person want to take action.

incumbent Person currently holding an office.

indecisiveness Inability to settle on a course of action.

indictments Formal charges against a person accused of a crime.

intervention Act of coming between two sides to settle or stop a dispute.

invigorating Filled with energy.

limekiln A furnace in which limestone, shells, etc., are burned to make lime used in mortar and cement.

negotiation Bargaining to reach agreement.

nurture Support, care for.

orator Speaker.

pampered Spoiled, indulged.

pilgrimage A long journey taken for a specific purpose, usually religious.

probation A period of supervision or evaluation.

reek Having a strong, unpleasant smell.

rehabilitate Restore to a former position or condition.

sideboard A piece of dining room furniture for holding table linens, silver, china, etc.

stagnant Not flowing or moving.

suffrage The right to vote.

suffragette A woman in the nineteenth century who worked for women's right to vote.

syndicated Refers to a group of newspapers that operate as a chain.

unscrupulous Paying no attention to what is right and honest.

valedictory Referring to the farewell speech delivered at graduation.

vaudeville A stage show made up of a variety of acts, including songs, dances, comedy skits, etc.

wayward Disobedient, stubborn.

Sources

CHAPTER ONE: Young Jane

p. 12, "My dear Mr. . . ." Jane Addams, *Twenty Years at Hull House* (New York: The New American Library, 1961), 20.

p. 18, "in the grip . . ." Ibid., 1-2.

p. 20, "had a little . . . sleep afterward" Ibid., 2.

p. 23, "why [do] people [live] . . ." Ibid.

CHAPTER TWO: Hearing Her Call

p. 28, "The greatest sorrow . . ." Marshall W. Fishwick et al., *Illustrious Americans: Jane Addams* (Morristown, NJ: Silver Burdett Company, 1968), 32.

p. 32, "It seems quite . . ." Gioia Diliberto, *A Useful Woman: The Early Life of Jane Addams* (New York: Scribner, 1999), 98.

p. 32, "I quite feel . . ." Allen F. Davis, *American Heroine: The Life and Legend of Jane Addams* (New York: Oxford University Press, 1973), 32.

p. 33, "He had bidden . . ." Addams, *Twenty Years,* 43.

p. 34, "I am simply . . ." Ibid., 47.

p. 34, "I have been idle . . ." Diliberto, *A Useful Woman,* 110.

p. 36, "cathedral of humanity . . ." Addams, *Twenty Years,* 53-54.

p. 38, "I had fallen . . ." Fishwick et al., *Illustrious Americans,* 40.

p. 40, "It [Toynbee Hall] . . ." Allen F. Davis and Mary Lynn McCree, eds., *Eighty Years at Hull House* (Chicago: Quadrangle Books, 1969), 19.

CHAPTER THREE: Building Hull House
p. 43, "The streets are . . ." Addams, *Twenty Years,* 64-65.
p. 49, "From the first . . ." Ibid., 72.
p. 50, "Goosie was always . . ." Ibid., 116.
p. 53, "It was open . . ." John C. Farrell, *Beloved Lady: A History of Jane Addams' Ideas on Reform and Peace* (Baltimore: The Johns Hopkins Press, 1967), 110-111.

CHAPTER FOUR: Social Justice
p. 54, "that they worked . . ." Addams, *Twenty Years,* 132.
p. 56, "An unscrupulous . . ." Jane Hovde, *Jane Addams* (New York: Facts on File, 1989), 46-47.
p. 57, "Many of the boys . . ." Ibid., 47.
p. 57, "I remember a little . . ." Addams, *Twenty Years,* 132.
p. 57, "From the age . . ." Diliberto, *A Useful Woman,* 178.
p. 60, "At least, the sweatshops . . ." Cornelia Meigs, *Jane Addams: Pioneer for Social Justice* (Boston: Little, Brown and Company, 1970), 142.
p. 62, "We are born . . ." Hovde, *Jane Addams,* 80.
p. 65, "lawbreaker at large . . ." Davis, *American Heroine,* 112.
p. 68, "I may well be . . ." Addams, *Twenty Years,* 187.

CHAPTER FIVE: Challenges and Growth
p. 72, "The trouble with . . ." Davis, *American Heroine,* 124.
p. 72, "I may not be . . ." Ibid., 125.
p. 75, "There was enough . . ." Ibid., 137.
p. 76, "Peace was not merely . . ." Jane Addams, *A Centennial Reader* (New York: The Macmillan Company, 1960), 251.
p. 76, "We care less . . ." Davis, *American Heroine,* 145.
p. 77, "I do not imagine . . ." Hovde, *Jane Addams,* 101.

p. 77, "practically the whole . . ." Ibid., 53.

p. 78, "It was the conception . . ." Meigs, *Jane Addams: Pioneer for Social Justice,* 154.

p. 80, "If I do it, I will . . ." James Weber Linn, *Jane Addams: A Biography* (Urbana: University of Illinois Press, 1935), 156.

CHAPTER SIX: The Progressives

p. 85, "Our schools must . . ." Fishwick et al., *Illustrious Americans,* 60.

p. 85, "My efforts were . . ." Linn, *Jane Addams: A Biography,* 232.

p. 87, "Your own people . . ." Fishwick et al., *Illustrious Americans,* 153.

p. 91, "Most of the departments . . ." Daniel Levine, *Jane Addams and the Liberal Tradition* (Madison: State Historical Society of Wisconsin, 1971), 182.

p. 91, "losing what they . . ." Hovde, *Jane Addams,* 93.

p. 91, "Women do not wish . . ." Ibid., 94.

p. 92, "Women who live . . ." Addams, *A Centennial Reader,* 105.

p. 94, "The Progressive . . ." Davis, *American Heroine,* 186.

p. 95, "A great party . . ." Levine, *Jane Addams and the Liberal Tradition,* 190-91.

p. 95, "Strong as a bull . . ." "Is It Time for a New Political Party?" *Time for Kids.* I. 4. Online. 6 Oct. 1995. www.timeforkids.com.

p. 96, "At that moment . . ." Levine, *Jane Addams and the Liberal Tradition,* 196.

p. 96, "I never doubted . . ." Davis, *American Heroine,* 186.

p. 97, "Wherever I went . . ." Ibid., 192.

CHAPTER SEVEN: Work for Peace

p. 100, "Jane Addams—don't . . ." Fishwick et al., *Illustrious Americans,* 69.

p. 100, "We, women of the . . ." Davis, *American Heroine,* 216-17.

p. 101, "women must show . . ." Ibid., 217.

p. 102, "Germany would not . . ." Farrell, *Beloved Lady,* 158.

p. 103, "Pacifists are cowards . . ." Fishwick et al., *Illustrious Americans,* 70.

p. 104, "Generally speaking . . ." Jean Bethke Elshtain, *Jane Addams and the Dream of American Democracy* (New York: Basic Books, 2002), 229.

p. 104, "not because of . . ." Ibid., 231.

p. 104, "delirious soldiers . . ." Fishwick et al., *Illustrious Americans,* 111.

p. 105, "Jane Addams is a silly . . ." Davis, *American Heroine,* 229.

p. 105, "Every nation . . ." Ibid., 230.

p. 107, "Out of the trenches . . ." Ibid., 238.

p. 108, "The situation [starvation] . . ." Farrell, *Beloved Lady,* 177.

p. 108, "In this great . . ." Addams, *A Centennial Reader,* 135.

p. 109, "The International Congress . . ." Meigs, *Jane Addams: Pioneer for Social Justice,* 225.

p. 110, "Our first impression . . ." Elshtain, *Jane Addams and the Dream of American Democracy,* 243.

p. 111, "I shall probably . . ." Linn, *Jane Addams: A Biography,* 340.

CHAPTER EIGHT: Most-Admired Woman

p. 114, "the most dangerous . . ." Davis, *American Heroine,* 25.

p. 114, "everybody who . . ." Ibid., 252-53.

p. 115, "I supposed . . ." Ibid., 85.

p. 115, "You know I am . . ." Fishwick et al., *Illustrious Americans,* 78.

p. 115, "In honoring Jane . . ." Davis, *American Heroine,* 268.

p. 115, "In a way I am . . ." Meigs, *Jane Addams: Pioneer for Social Justice,* 245.

p. 116, "She has lost . . ." Davis, *American Heroine,* 269.

p. 116, "In 1912 I learned . . ." Linn, *Jane Addams: A Biography,*

347-48.

p. 118, "the twelve greatest . . ." Ibid., 380.

p. 118, "To Alice Hamilton . . ." Meigs, *Jane Addams: Pioneer for Social Justice,* 259.

p. 120, "In honoring Jane . . ." Halvdan Koht. Presentation Speech, Nobel Peace Prize, 1931. www.nobel.se/peace/laureates/1931/press.html.

p. 122, "In every dark hour . . ." Fishwick et al., *Illustrious Americans,* 82.

p. 122, "Jane Addams really . . ." Ibid.

p. 123, "It is really . . ." Davis, *American Heroine,* 288.

p. 123, "willingness to learn . . ." Fishwick et al., *Illustrious Americans,* 87.

p. 123, "It is for being . . ." Farrell, *Beloved Lady,* 214.

p. 124, "We don't expect . . ." Elshtain, *Jane Addams and the Dream of American Democracy,* 247.

p. 124, "When I was a child . . ." Linn, *Jane Addams: A Biography,* 420-21.

p. 127, "I think of her . . ." Fishwick et al., *Illustrious Americans,* 88.

p. 127, "She had compassion . . ." Elshtain, *Jane Addams and the Dream of American Democracy,* 249.

Bibliography

Addams, Jane. *A Centennial Reader.* New York: The Macmillan Company, 1960.

———. *Twenty Years at Hull House.* New York: The New American Library, Inc., 1961.

Davis, Allen F. *American Heroine: The Life and Legend of Jane Addams.* New York: Oxford University Press, 1973.

Davis, Allen F., and Mary Lynn McCree, eds. *Eighty Years at Hull House.* Chicago: Quadrangle Books, 1969.

Diliberto, Gioia. *A Useful Woman: The Early Life of Jane Addams.* New York: Scribner, 1999.

Elshtain, Jean Bethke. *Jane Addams and the Dream of American Democracy.* New York: Basic Books, 2002.

Farrell, John C. *Beloved Lady: A History of Jane Addams' Ideas on Reform and Peace.* Baltimore: The Johns Hopkins Press, 1967.

Fishwick, Marshall W. et al. *Illustrious Americans: Jane Addams.* Morristown, NJ: Silver Burdett Company, 1968.

Hovde, Jane. *Jane Addams.* New York: Facts on File, 1989.

Is It Time for a New Political Party?" *Time for Kids.* I. 4. 6 Oct. 1995. http://www.timeforkids.com

Koht, Halvdan. Presentation Speech, Nobel Peace Prize 1931. http://www.Nobel.se/peace/laureates/1931/press.html.

Levine, Daniel. *Jane Addams and the Liberal Tradition*. Madison: State Historical Society of Wisconsin, 1971.

Linn, James Weber. *Jane Addams: A Biography*. Urbana: University of Illinois Press, 1935.

Meigs, Cornelia. *Jane Addams: Pioneer for Social Justice*. Boston: Little, Brown and Company, 1970.

Web sites:

The Jane Addams Collection at Swarthmore College
**www.swarthmore.edu/Library/peace/Exhibits/janeaddams/
addamsindex.html**
Offers a brief biography of Jane Addams, many photographs, and links to other areas within the Swarthmore Peace Collection.

The Jane Addams Hull House Association
www.hullhouse.org/
Provides a history of the organization, information on community programs the association offers, and related news and events.

The Jane Addams Hull-House Museum
www.uic.edu/jaddams/hull/hull_house.html
This site has an extensive biography of Jane Addams, detailed timeline, photos, and links to extremely useful and informative site on the urban experience in Chicago.

The Nobel Peace Prize Web site
www.nobel.se/peace/laureates/1931/index.html
Focusing on the year Jane Addams received the prize, with links to other years and additional prizewinners.

Index